M000084496

ARGENTINA

A WOMAN'S GUIDE TO TRAVELING IN ARGENTINA

Go! Girl Guides makes every attempt to help you travel safely and affordably; however, we do not assume responsibility or liability arising from the use of this book, and make no warranty about the accuracy of its content.

Have we made a mistake? Let us know by emailing info@gogirlguides.com

No part of this book may be copied, stored, or transmitted without written permission of the publisher.

Go! Girl Guides: Argentina First Edition
Published by Go! Girl Travel LLC, Tucson, Arizona.
© 2012 All Rights Reserved.

Library of Congress Control Number: 2012945717

Layout, Design, & Illustration:
John H. Clark IV and Alyson Kilday
HOP & JAUNT Creative Agency
www.hopandjaunt.com

Maps Courtesy of:
Ministry of Tourism Argentina
www.turismo.gov.ar

Cover Photo:
Erica Arvizu
Puerto Iguazu waterfalls

CONTENTS

ABOUT   1

SAFETY   9

HEALTH   23

BEFORE YOU GO   37

CULTURE AND CUSTOMS   57

BUENOS AIRES   73

CÓRDOBA   97

CENTRAL   105

NORTHEAST   123

NORTH (SALTA)   137

NORTH (JUJUY)   155

PATAGONIA   173

CUYO   211

VOLUNTEER   225

FOOD AND RECIPES   233

Q&As   249

LANGUAGE   257

INDEX   265

TOURIST MAP
www.argentina.travel

Since 1981 Argentina has been distinguished by UNESCO several times; many areas within its territory have been declared World Natural and Cultural Heritage Sites

WORLD HERITAGES

QUEBRADA DE HUMAHUACA

Province of Jujuy
World Cultural Landscape

The Quebrada de Humahuaca's multicolored landscape frame the villages of Purmamarca, Maimará, Tilcara and Humahuaca.
Its adobe houses, historical chapels and Pre-Hispanic ruins provide a stunning view.
A monolith marks the Tropic of Capricorn, where each June 21st, the celebration of the Inti Raymi (Sun Festival) takes place.

IGUAZÚ NATIONAL PARK

Province of Misiones
World Natural Heritage Site

The famous Iguazú Falls, one of the most spectacular waterfalls in the world, are at the heart of this National Park. An impressive amount of water plunges 70m into the abyss below, breaking into 270 cataracts and drops.
The border between Argentina and Brazil is marked by the Garganta del Diablo (Devil's Throat) drop.
The surrounding park has over 2000 species of plants and is home to the region's exotic wildlife, including more than 400 bird species.

JESUIT MISSIONS OF THE GUARANIS

Province of Misiones
World Cultural Heritage Site

Jesuit Missions of the Guaraní Natives San Ignacio Miní, Nuestra Señora de Loreto, Santa Ana and Santa María la Mayor. Jesuit Missions constitute a 396 km long tourist itinerary of incredible scenic beauty.
These reductions, settled in Argentina in the 17th century, were part of the 30 villages that formed the Ancient Jesuit Province of Paraguay.

ISCHIGUALASTO AND TALAMPAYA NATURAL PARKS

Provinces of San Juan and La Rioja
World Natural Heritage Site

The Ischigualasto Provincial Park (San Juan), also known as Moon Valley is one of the greatest paleontological reserves of the world, rich in remains of vertebrates from the Mesozoic Era and early dinosaur footprints, and the Talampaya National Park (La Rioja), with cliffs and reddish rock formations that are the perching place for Andean condors, are situated in a 5,000 sq. km basin. Petroglyphs of uncertain origin and age are one of Talampaya's astounding features, along with the massive walls, over 150 meters high, of the 3 km long canyon.

JESUIT BLOCK AND ESTANCIAS OF CÓRDOBA

Province of Córdoba
World Cultural Heritage Site

This magnificent collection of historical buildings include the Church of the Compañía de Jesús, the elegant Capilla Doméstica, the Jesuits Residence and the Rectorate of Córdoba National University, together with the University Council, Confirming Rooms, the Higher Library and the Monserrat National High School. The Jesuit Estancias Jesús María, Caroya, Santa Catalina, La Candelaria and Alta Gracia are visited in a 250 km itinerary following a hilly landscape.

PENÍNSULA VALDÉS

Province of Chubut
World Natural Heritage Site

Two gulfs of Península Valdés, San José and Nuevo, are the meeting points of the Southern Right Whales. They gather here every year between May and December to feed and breed. The fauna concentration in this area is outstanding: Elephant seals, sea lions, and Magellanic penguins, as well as guanacos (Lama guanicoe, a relative of the Andean llama) and rheas (Rhea's relatives patagónica), also known as Patagonian hare. The Isla de los Pájaros reserve protects thousands of bird species.

CUEVA DE LAS MANOS AT THE UPPER PINTURAS RIVER

Province of Santa Cruz
World Cultural Heritage Site

Located South of the Perito Moreno town, by the Alto Río Pinturas Valley, the Cueva de las Manos (Cave of the Hands) contains one of the most significant assemblages of cave art in the Patagonia. Vestiges of a 9,000 year old culture are found in the caves and the gully's rocky sides, which show stenciled outlines of human hands and other rich pre-historic depictions giving testimony to its past.

LOS GLACIARES NATIONAL PARK

Province of Santa Cruz
World Natural Heritage Site

Thirteen glaciers, all of them feeding into the Atlantic basin, break into huge towers of ice over the Viedma and Argentino lakes. The front walls of the Perito Moreno, Mayo, Spegazzini and Upsala glaciers topple into the Argentino lake waters.
The glaciers may be visited via a boat trip for a closer view of this breath-taking natural wonder.
El Calafate, which has an airport, is the closest urban center.

ARGENTINA INVITES YOU

Distances
from City of Buenos Aires (Km)

A NOTE FROM THE EDITOR

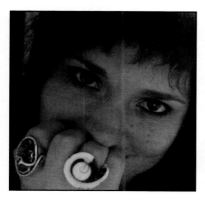

Argentina is the eighth largest country in the world and one of the most diverse, offering everything from deep blue glaciers to multicolored mountains and barren deserts.

Large cities like Buenos Aires seduce travelers with promises of tango and steak dinners, beckoning all who go there to lose themselves in the sights and sounds of the large metropolis.

Outside of the cities, you'll find a gorgeous and often untouched world that's full of llamas, penguins, waterfalls, small villages, friendly people, wine, and of course, more steak.

There are a million reasons to fall in love with Argentina, but traveling the country does not come without its challenges. Argentina is still firmly rooted in *machismo* culture, and it can be difficult for your voice to be heard, especially in stressful situations. You will undoubtedly experience catcalls from love-struck men, likely on the day you least feel like dealing with it. There may also be times when you feel like everything is much more complicated than it should be, and days when you're sure that the locals are giving you the runaround by offering you 10 different directions to the grocery store.

With this book, we hope to help you travel safely and easily through this large, meat-loving paradise. It took us the combined experience of six trips to do this guide justice, so you can be sure that we'll give you sound advice on everything from riding the bus across the country to renting an apartment in Buenos Aires.

Whether you're here to eat, to learn, to volunteer, to shop or to do all of the above, Argentina has a little bit of something to keep you hooked and coming back for more.

--Kelly Lewis, Editor-in-Chief

Kelly Lewis
Editor-in-Chief
GGG Founder

Erica Arvizu
Co-Author

Page Buono
Co-Author

ABOUT

···· WHO WE ARE AND HOW TO USE THE BOOK ····

Go! Girl Guides was created from a dream in early 2011. As seasoned travelers ourselves, we couldn't understand why there weren't resources that addressed the specific needs of solo travelin' gals—so we made one.

In this book, you'll find information that's tailor-made just for *you*, lady, and we left no stone unturned. You'll get information on safe and inexpensive places to stay, read about common scams to be aware of, find out where to buy tampons and how to get birth control. We want you to stay safe while traveling, and have a blast, too.

We scoured the country to find the best budget accommodation in the country, and whenever possible, we'll tell you how to get there using public transportation. Primarily, we looked for safe places—clean guesthouses and hostels in good neighborhoods that provide safety deposit boxes, security cameras, key-card access, or have female-only dorms. We saw dozens of ramshackle places that we'd never want to step foot in again … all so you don't have to.

The world is a very inviting place, and Argentina is no exception.

Get inspired to get out there with first-hand tips from fellow female travelers in our Q&A section, cook up a storm with the Food and Recipe section, and find out how to give back during your travels with our Volunteer section, which features only free or low-cost organizations that operate throughout Argentina.

**We believe that travel can be both stimulating and affordable.
We believe in adventures that change lives.
We believe that every woman has the power to do extraordinary things.**

…and we know you do too. So, what are you waiting for?

www.gogirlguides.com

EDITOR-IN-CHIEF

Kelly Lewis

Founder of Go! Girl Guides, Kelly is a writer, a dreamer and an avid traveler. Originally from Hawaii, Kelly lived in New Zealand for a year before traversing through South America and the South Pacific. She started Go! Girl Guides in late 2010 after it came to her in a dream.

AUTHORS

Erica Arvizu

Erica has been working in and out of newsrooms for the past five years. Her passion for journalism and Spanish, as well as an itch to see the world, made her the perfect fit for this venture. Traveling solo through Argentina for this guidebook has given her the travel bug, and this is hopefully her first of many jaunts abroad.

Page Buono

After graduating from Western Washington University's journalism program, Page bounced around the U.S. for a bit before landing an internship with the United Nations Refugee Agency in Uganda, where she spent nearly a year working with and writing about refugees in and around Uganda. After co-authoring this book, she decided to stay in Argentina and is now living on an estancia in Northern Patagonia, drinking obscene amounts of maté, riding horses, and learning more about los gauchos while plotting her next move.

CONTRIBUTORS

Traci Salisbury
Traci has been writing for Go! Girl Guides online for the past year, and recently traveled solo across Central and South America. She wrote the Mendoza section found in this guidebook, contributed photos and added to our volunteer section.

Big thank you's go out to editors Chase Gilbert and Justyn Dillingham for catching our stupid mistakes and Hop & Jaunt Creative Agency for their stellar design work.

THANK YOU

The following individuals are owed giant thank you's for their support with our Kickstarter campaign, which helped us create this guidebook.

Allie Baron, Karen Kahn, Adessa, Kevin Mills, Becki Robichaud, Jaclynn, Molly Leibowitz, Bettina Silverman, Kristin Hovanec, Clare Wilson, David, Vanessa, Tara Shea, Katie Daubert, Devon Frederickson, John Moritz, Karen Holmes, Justyn Dillingham, Chase Gilbert, Niklas Morris

SAFETY

TRAVELING SOLO DOES NOT
MEAN YOU'RE ALONE

Here at Go! Girl Guides we believe that women should feel empowered, enthusiastic and excited to take on world travel, and we know you do too.

So why does it seem like many of our well-meaning friends and family are completely opposed to the idea of us traveling solo?

They probably just don't understand: traveling solo doesn't mean you're alone.

These days it's so easy to meet up with other travelers while on the road that you may find you are very rarely, well, *alone*.

At some point on your journey you will no doubt find yourself in conversations with other travelers while in the airport, on buses, boats, trains and subways—and that's before you even make it to the hostel.

After a while, you may even become exhausted with the standard traveler's conversation: *Where are you from? Where are you headed? Where have you been?*

And still yet, you'll see that many of these conversations end up giving you tidbits of useful information such as where to stay, where to eat and how to score a cheap room.

So how can you reassure the naysayers that traveling solo is both safe, and awesome? Where can you meet more people?

Couchsurfing.org
Make plans to check out the community meetings in your city of choice, find a place to crash, connect with some cool people,

or just post your travel itinerary in a group discussion and see if anyone wants to join you—and they probably will!

Hostels
Even if you book a private room, all you have to do to meet people at hostels is make yourself available and open. Hang out in common rooms, cook in the kitchen. Hostels are wonderful places to meet members of the backpacking community, find travel buddies and swap stories.

·············· RESOURCES TO USE TO STAY SAFE ··············

There are a ton of resources you can use to help you stay safe while traveling. Community forums like Couchsurfing.org provide great places to meet and connect with other travelers, but here are some more resources for you to consider.

Note: While this information is valid for U.S. citizens traveling abroad, check with your local embassy for emergency numbers and traveler's assistance programs.

Smart Traveler Enrollment Program
The Smart Traveler Enrollment Program is a free online program through the U.S. Department of State and is available to all U.S. citizens. In giving them your travel plans, the agency will be able to contact you if there is an emergency at home or in the country where you are traveling. They also give expats information on nearby consulates and embassies.

Sign up at *travelregistration.state.gov*.

Center for Disease Control International Travelers Information
The CDC provides information on diseases and prevention for travelers, but cannot diagnose. Call 1-800-CDC-INFO for more information, and follow the prompts for "International Travelers Information."

Consulates
Consular personnel are available 24/7 for U.S. citizens in the event of an emergency. To call The Office of Overseas Citizens Services, call 1-888-407-4747 or 202-647-5225 after hours. You can find a list of overseas embassies and consulates at *www.state.gov/countries*.

EMERGENCY NUMBERS

Tourist Police: Dial +011 4346-5748 / 0800-999-5000. Tourist police are available in most every region, 24/7.

Police/Emergency: 101 (For Salta, Buenos Aires, Santa Fe and Rosario, you can also call 911)

Firemen: 100

Ambulance: 107

EMERGENCY NUMBERS:

POLICE / EMERGENCY: 101
FIRE: 100
AMBULANCE: 107
TOURIST POLICE:
+011 4346-5748 / 0800-999-5000

TOURIST POLICE UNIT

The Argentine Federal Police have established a special Tourist Police Unit to receive complaints and investigate crimes against tourists. The unit, located at Corrientes 436 in Buenos Aires, responds to calls around the clock at 4346-5748 or toll-free 0800-999-5000 from anywhere in the country. The Mendoza Tourist Police Unit, open 7 a.m. to 10 p.m. daily, is located at San Martin 1143, telephone 0261-413-2135. After hours, the Mendoza unit may be reached by cell phone at 0261-15-6444-324.

TIPS ON HOW TO STAY SAFE
AND GET THE MOST OUT OF YOUR TRIP

These basic tips will help you navigate Argentina safely, and the rest of the world:

Drink, But Don't Get Drunk
Feel free to enjoy yourself and indulge a little bit, but don't get too crazy. It's best to be able to keep your wits about you, especially when you're out at night. Plus, alcohol is expensive in Argentina, and those drinks add up!

Avoid Drugs
Don't you remember what happened to Claire Danes in "Brokedown Palace"? Avoid drugs while traveling in other countries and never transport them. If you're getting on a bus somewhere, double-check to make sure that you aren't carrying anything illegal in case you encounter a checkpoint. There are always checkpoints up north near the Bolivian border.

Pre-Plan
While half of the fun of traveling is not having a plan, sometimes it's good to know at least the basics: where you're going, and where you're going to sleep. Once you have that down, the rest is a breeze.

Use Radio Taxis in Buenos Aires
Radio taxis are regulated in Argentina, so they're your best bet. Check to see that the taxi says "Radio Taxi" on the side before getting in. If you have a bill larger than 50 pesos, ask the driver if he can break it before accepting a ride.

Learn and Speak Spanish
There are many places where you don't necessarily need to speak Spanish, but other places where it will be very hard to get around without it. Speaking Spanish can only help you. You'll be able to talk to locals and get involved in conversations, learn about culture without needing a translator, effectively negotiate in markets, read menus in restaurants, get directions if you're lost, ask for recommendations, easily get around cities and towns and earn some respect from locals with your language skills. If you're looking to get off the backpacker trail and have some adventures, Spanish is the key.

Walk With Purpose

If you take a wrong turn and feel unsafe in a particular neighborhood, walk with purpose towards a business or hotel to ask for directions, or hop in a taxi. It's important to remember that the people of Argentina are generally warm, helpful, and not out to get you, but listen to your instincts if you feel unsafe and ask for help.

Don't Flaunt It

Wearing flashy, gaudy, or expensive jewelry draws attention to you, as does overly revealing clothing. Dress conservatively and keep your accessories to a minimum, unless it's jewelry you've bought locally. Be especially aware of this while traveling through smaller towns in the north, and while in the neighborhood of La Boca in Buenos Aires.

Go With Your Gut

Feel uncomfortable or uneasy in a particular situation? Always listen to your gut. You're in charge of whom you spend your time with, how much you reveal about yourself, where you go and how you get there. Remember that a direct, but polite "no, thank you" is always in your realm of possibility.

Keep in Touch at Home

Call your family each time you touch down in a new town or city to let them know you're safe. If you plan to stay in one spot for an extended period of time, check in at least once a week. Internet is available practically everywhere in Argentina, so you'll always be able to Skype, and your family will appreciate it. We promise.

Ignore Catcalls

As a female traveler, you may run into some machismo during your travels, such as catcalls or whistles. Uncomfortable? Yes, but almost always harmless. It's best to ignore advances and continue on your way (walking with purpose, of course), but if you feel threatened at any time, head into a business or store and ask for help or wait for them to pass.

Some useful phrases if you get stuck:

A forceful "*no*."
"*Dejame en paz.*" Leave me in peace.
"*Basta.*" Enough.
"*No me toques.*" Don't touch me.

Just for the record, we never had to use any of these phrases during our travels, but it's always best to be prepared.

When Asking For Directions, Get a Few Opinions

For whatever reason, when asking for directions on the street, sometimes people will tell you they know the place you're looking for even if they don't. Our best guess as to why this happens is simply because they don't want to say no—the people of Argentina are that polite. Always walk a block and ask again. It's not that locals purposefully try to steer you the wrong way—most of the time, they're happy to help—but if someone seems unsure, it's likely you're not going to find your destination off their directions. Get a few responses before heading very far.

·············· HOW TO DEAL WITH CATCALLS ················

Argentina is a beautiful country, but the men? Well, the men can be a bit … forward. If you're foreign and traveling through South America, chances are you'll encounter catcalls, or *piropos*, via the whistling, yelling, or gross kissy noises that men will throw your way. It doesn't matter if you look like a hot, sweaty, disheveled mess—you're female.

Machismo culture, or the belief that men are totally dominant, is prevalent here, but that doesn't mean you can't find ways to combat the catcalls and keep yourself safe. Before you get all worked up, remember: they're not trying to disrespect you, it's a cultural thing.

Here are some tips on how to deal with catcalls:

Don't Respond

When you're being hit on, keep your head down and walk away. Making eye contact will often add more fuel to the fire, and give them more of an incentive to try to talk to you.

Don't Fall for the Lines

Oh, you'll get them all. Cheesy lines like: "I love you," "you're so beautiful," and "I never knew heaven until I saw you" may come up in conversation. Barf! If you're not into it, politely smile, end your conversation, and walk away.

Remember You're Not From Here
Keep it all in perspective. This is a different country, and things are done differently here. Before you grab your mace and start swinging fists in response to a catcall, remember that this is something you just have to deal with. Just keep walking.

Learn Some Slang
If you're all fired up from a catcall, throw out a few choice words. "*Che, boludo*" or "*¡No me toques!*" if they try to touch you. "*¡Déjame en paz!*" (leave me in peace) should also do the trick.

Be Aware and Be Careful
If you're walking late at night and you hear something, speed-walk yourself to safety. If absolutely necessary, duck into a restaurant or a corner store and wait it out for a few minutes.

RIDING THE BUS ACROSS ARGENTINA: WHAT TO KNOW

As far as public transportation goes, Argentina's bus lines are among some of the best in the world. Though the hours may be long (more than 24 hours in some cases) you will likely be in a comfortable seat with room to stretch your legs, there will be movies playing, and they'll feed you.

Here's a rundown of what to know before you board the bus.

Tickets

- Purchase tickets directly from the bus station. Day-of tickets are available, but it's best to buy your ticket at least 24 hours in advance, or more if you're traveling on a national holiday.

- Shop around between bus companies to find the best rate. Most will be cash-only.

- Your options for seats will be cama or semi-cama—cama being a reclining seat that is easier to sleep in. If you can afford it, cama is the most desirable and will give you the most space. If not, semi-cama is comfortable as well.

Before You Board

- Your ticket will usually tell you which numbered space your bus will depart from, e.g., #18-23. You won't know exactly where the bus will pull up until it does, so you'll need to keep an eye out around the time of departure and read signs on the buses to know which one you need to get on.

- If in doubt, ask someone—either at your company's ticketing office at the bus station, or one of the locals waiting to board.

On Board

- Food: If you're going on a long ride, you'll likely be fed. Usually, this will consist of a ham and cheese sandwich, juice or water and a dessert. Bring snacks to hold you over if you think you'll be hungry.

- Movies will be shown, but they may or may not be in English.

- There should be a toilet on board. Bring your own toilet paper!

Safety

- If you're feeling nervous about riding the bus, try to get a seat at the front, near the driver.

- If traveling alone, be wary of engaging in conversation with the men on the bus, particularly bus employees. If they are local, they may assume you're single—and therefore available.

- Do not leave your bag on the floor of the bus. Hold it in your lap, use it as a pillow, or keep it very close to you. If you get off the bus for a stop, bring it with you.

- Your large pack will likely be placed under the bus. Be sure to take out valuables and keep them in a small bag with you (along with a change of clothes, just in case).

Other Tips

Arrive at least 20 minutes before your bus departs. Don't panic if it's a little late!

BEWARE OF BUS EMPLOYEES

We hate that we even have to say this, but, while traveling through Argentina, it's very common for women to have negative experiences with the male employees who work on the bus lines. Why? When you're on a bus for 30 hours, they're in a position of power.

If a bus employee offers you a better seat and then uses it as a chance to sit next to you and harass you, politely go back to your original seat. If you're using the bathroom on a bus, check the walls and doors to make sure there are no holes. GGG Founder Kelly was spied on once while using the bathroom on a bus to Patagonia. When she caught the employee red-handed, she wrote an official complaint form, but, of course, nothing was ever done.

To avoid being in a sticky situation while on a bus in Argentina, try not to interact too much with the employees. Making eye contact and engaging in conversations can sometimes send the signal that you're interested, even if you're not.

MACHISMO CULTURE AND HOW IT WILL AFFECT YOU

Listen up, ladies: machismo culture, or the belief that men are in charge, is the common belief in Argentina and you'll have to find ways to deal with it. It's an unfortunate side of traveling, but it shouldn't be taken personally. After all, this is not your country and things are done differently here.

Here's an idea of how machismo culture will inevitably affect you, and what you can do to make traveling easier.

Scenario 1: You get into a situation in which a man violates your space. You become extremely offended and start talking to authorities in charge, but no one seems to care.

How to Deal: It's frustrating, but common—your voice may not be heard the way you want it to be. If you're in a situation like this, remain calm. Speak slowly, softly and use emotion. If you're affected to the point of tears, others will take notice, but don't expect anyone to come to your rescue. Compose yourself, and do all you can to explain the situation to the proper authorities.

Scenario 2: You go out to dinner with a man, but he won't let you order.

How to Deal: It's common for men to do the ordering for women at restaurants. If you have a dietary restriction, explain this to your date ahead of time. If you have to, find the wait staff after the order has been placed and do your best to explain what you really want.

Scenario 3: You're unmarried, but in a relationship. Yet, the advances just keep coming.

How to Deal: For whatever reason, having a significant other is of little importance to Argentine men, unless you're married, and saying "I have a boyfriend" may be akin to "I have a cat." Frustrating, but true. The best thing you can do in this situation is to move yourself away from who is hitting on you, and offer a clear and direct "No."

········ HOW TO PROTECT YOUR BELONGINGS ········

Staying in shared hostel rooms, traveling by bus, taking public transportation and walking through crowds with valuables can be somewhat nerve-racking if you're not prepared. Here are some tips on keeping your belongings safe:

• Stay in hostels with lockers and pack a small lock. Use it every-where you stay to lock up your valuables. If something doesn't fit in your locker, store it somewhere safely out of sight, such as under your pillow or between the sheets.

• Only leave electronics to charge when you're in the room.

• Split up large sums of money into different compartments of your carry on and backpack. That way, if someone takes some pesos, it won't be all of them. When traveling between destinations, wear a money belt and keep your passport, credit cards, and the majority of your cash inside.

• Your purse or day-bag should have a zipper. The most practical bags can be worn cross-body. Keep your bag in front of your person and zipped shut. Be aware of where it hangs when you are on public transportation and walking through large crowds.

- When traveling on buses, keep your carry-on bag on your lap or in front of your feet. There are overhead spaces for storage, but keeping it in your line of sight makes it harder to take.

Don't be paranoid—be cautious! Common sense is the most powerful weapon you have against theft.

COMMON SCAMS AND HOW TO AVOID THEM

Pickpockets
Around the world, the pickpocket is the easiest way to come up on cash, phones, electronics, and whatever else is within easy reach of a distracted target. The best way to avoid getting pickpocketed is to keep your bag in front of your body, zipped shut. When walking through dense crowds or packed public transportation, keep your free hand over the zipper and your gaze alert. Pickpockets are usually not seen or heard, and the easiest targets are the ones who are not paying attention.

Purses with interior compartments are also a great way to prevent pickpockets. The harder it is to get to your cash, camera, phone, etc., the less likely it is that anything will be stolen.

The Mustard Trick
Thieves squirt something on you, resembling mustard. When you notice it, someone suddenly rushes over to help you clean it, quickly ridding you of your things. If something spills on you from above, or if something is squirted at you, calmly continue on without stopping. This is a common scam around the Retiro bus station in Buenos Aires.

"Miss, Miss, Visit This Bar"
Sometimes, scammers entice travelers into bars with fliers for free shows or free drinks. Once inside, they will not allow you to leave without paying a fee. It's hard to get around this. If you're ever in this situation, there's little you can do but pay the fee and move on. Trust your gut.

The Slashed Bag
In bigger cities around large, crowded tourist attractions and on

public transportation, unsuspecting people sometimes have their purses cut open by an anonymous thief standing behind them.

Once the hole is cut, everything inside is on the ground and can quickly be snatched up by the thief. The best way to avoid this is to carry your bag in front of your body and hold it there until you're away from the crowd. The easiest bags to cut are made out of cloth, so consider something more sturdy, such as leather, if you're planning a big day of sightseeing.

MODESTY IS THE BEST POLICY

Buenos Aires is one of the world's leading fashion capitals, but Argentina as a whole is still a largely conservative country. Now, no one is going to throw rocks at you for wearing shorts, but if you're traveling through smaller towns or are on a bus for a long time, it's best to cover up a bit to avoid unwanted attention.

It's also a showing of respect that will get you a lot further in making local friends.

U.S. EMBASSIES AND CONSULATES

The only U.S. Embassy in Argentina is located in Buenos Aires. For a listing of other embassies in Argentina, visit *www.embassy.goabroad.com/embassies-in/argentina*.

Av. Colombia 4300
(C1425GMN) Buenos Aires
Argentina
+54 115-777-4533
www.argentina.usembassy.gov

HEALTH

Dra. Claudia María Battista
Av. Santa Fe 1675 2 floor, Apt. "A"
Recoleta, Buenos Aires
4815-4802 or 15-4448-4733
Language: English
claudiabattista@fibertel.com.ar

Dra. Gisela Beraud de Ahuad
Av. R. Scalabrini Ortiz 2433 1st floor, Apt. "A"
Palermo, Buenos Aires
4831-1318 or 4804-4720
Language: English
ahuad@tibo.com.ar

Dra. Pamela Brein
Av. Pueyrredón 1364 2nd floor, Apt. "D"
Recoleta, Buenos Aires
4822-5807 or 4829-9301
Language: English
pbrein@fibertel.com.ar

Dra. María Mónica Calloni
Arcos 2289 4th floor, Apt. "B"
Belgrano – Colegiales, Buenos Aires
4781-4612 or 4786-9115
Language: English
mcalloni@arnet.com.ar

Dra. Liliana Beatriz Campos
Marcelo T. de Alvear 2345 4th floor, Apt. "B"
Recoleta, Buenos Aires
4826-0209 or 4823-9058
Language: English

··· VACCINATIONS AND REQUIRED MEDICINES ···

It's recommended that you see a doctor four to six weeks before your date of travel to allow time for vaccinations and medications to take proper effect. You can find a list of vaccination clinics at the International Society of Travel Medicine, _www.istm.org_.

The Center for Disease Control recommends the following vaccinations:

- Routine vaccinations, including measles, mumps, rubella and tetanus
- Hepatitis A
- Hepatitis B
- Typhoid
- Yellow Fever

················ MALARIA AND DENGUE FEVER ················

You're traveling to a new country, so don't freak out if you get an upset stomach due to the new things you're eating. If you experience these symptoms for longer than 24 hours, however, it's time to visit the nearest doctor's office or hospital.

Dengue Fever
Symptoms of Dengue Fever include severe headache, pain behind the eyes, joint and muscle pain, rashes, nausea/vomiting, fever and hemorrhagic (bleeding) manifestations. Dengue Fever is commonly contracted in lush jungles and near areas with stagnant water.

Malaria
Malaria is very rare but there have been reported cases within the Salta province near the border with Bolivia and near Puerto Iguazu. No cases have been transmitted at Iguazu Falls. The likelihood that you would contract Malaria while in Argentina is very low, but if you experience the following symptoms, visit a hospital immediately: Fever, chills, sweats, headache, body aches, and nausea and vomiting, fatigue.

The most common way to contract both Dengue Fever and Malaria is through mosquito bites. Here are a few tips to reduce your risks of being bitten:

- Make sure that mosquito repellent is applied as a final step in skin care (e.g., after you have applied lotion or sunscreen).

- The EPA-approved and CDC-recommended ingredients to look for in repellent are: DEET, Picaridin, and oil of lemon eucalyptus. We recommend Repel Lemon Eucalyptus Pump Insect Repellent. It contains 40 percent of the active ingredient that wards off mosquitoes. Keep in mind that you will need to follow the instructions on the bottle to know how often it needs to be applied.

- Reduce the amount of skin that you're flashing. This also provides the added convenience of attracting less attention from unwanted human admirers.

- Seek out hotels and hostels that have air-conditioning and proper screens.

PREGNANCY

Abortions are illegal in Argentina, except in instances of rape or when the pregnancy puts a woman's health at risk, and even then may be unattainable legally. Unsafe abortions, legal or not, do occur, which puts women at great risk.

The International Planned Parenthood Federation for the Western Hemisphere Region works in Argentina and continues to fight for increased education, advocacy and women's rights in the country.

"The health exception is one of the components of legal permission for the termination of a pregnancy guaranteed by the majority of Latin American and Caribbean countries. This exception refers to the possibility of terminating a pregnancy when the pregnancy puts the woman's health at risk. However, its practical implementation has been accompanied by a combination of obstacles that have resulted in many women not accessing safe and timely abortion services, even when legally permitted."

– International Planned Parenthood Federation for the Western Hemisphere Region.

BIRTH CONTROL

While a bit hard to find, birth control is available in Argentina. However, some pharmacies require a prescription, while others do not. To obtain birth control easily, bring your current medication with you, including that small white packet of information that comes in every case. If you're going to be in the country for an extended period of time, visit one of the above-suggested gynecologists when you get into the country, as navigating the system with their assistance is much easier. Be sure to check the expiration date on birth control (or any medication, for that matter) as 40,000 expired IUD's were recalled in Argentina in 2009 after they were reported ineffective.

Morning-after pill
Commonly referred to as "*pastilla de dia despues*," the morning-after pill is available in most pharmacies for between 30 and 40 pesos. There are two different types, one is a one-dose pill and the other is two doses. Both are effective and cost roughly the same. Here is a list of brands of progestin-only ECPs (the brand most common in the states is Plan B).

Norgestrel Max
Ovulol
Postinor-1
Postinor-2

Condoms
Condoms are widely available in pharmacies, grocery stores and kioskos, or kiosks. You may get a few weird looks when you buy them, especially if a male clerk is ringing you up, but push on through! Your health is more important than a minute of embarrassment. If you feel uncomfortable, just stick to purchasing them through pharmacies.

SEXUALLY TRANSMITTED DISEASES

The most frequently reported STDs in Argentina are trichomoniasis, chlamydia, gonorrhea, herpes, syphilis, HPV, chancroid and HIV/AIDS. Just be smart girls, that's all we're sayin'.

TAMPONS

You can usually find tampons in large grocery stores like Disco, Coto, Jumbo and Carrefour, but your preferred brand may not be available. Smaller mom-and-pop local grocery stores are hit and miss. Some will have them, but most will not. It can be more difficult to find tampons outside of Buenos Aires. Sanitary napkins are available nearly everywhere.

TOILET PAPER

While most restrooms in restaurants and cafes provide toilet paper, it is not uncommon for them to run out, and public restrooms almost never have any. In many restrooms, the toilet paper is located outside of the stalls, so keep your eyes out. Occasionally you may be asked to pay for toilet paper, but it is usually less than 1 peso.

Keep a little toilet paper with you when you go out, but remember to put it in the trash can, not down the toilet.

TRAVELING TO REMOTE AREAS? STOCK UP!

You can find almost anything you need in Buenos Aires. But if you are traveling to more remote parts of the north or south, stock up on feminine products before you take off as they can be hard to find in some more rural locations. This goes for birth control, tampons and the morning-after pill as well.

NAVIGATING AN ARGENTINE PHARMACY

You can generally find anything you need at a pharmacy in Argentina, from razor blades to birth control, as long as you know how to ask for it. Most pharmacies will operate solely in Spanish, except for a few of the larger pharmacies within Buenos Aires. Unless you know the medicinal name for the prescription you're seeking, you'll have to describe your symptoms or what you're looking for to the pharmacist behind the counter.

More often than not, you'll need to have these conversations in Spanish, so come prepared—look up translations online for the symptoms you're experiencing, or ask your hostel staff if they know the name of the medicine you're seeking. In some nicer pharmacies, you may be able to tell the pharmacist the name of your medicine in English and they can look it up. This technology is not present in all pharmacies.

Keep in mind that several pharmacies close throughout the day for siestas, and many will not be open past 3 p.m. Many stores are also closed on Sundays. Pharmacies within large strip malls or business centers may have the best hours.

Some common women's health medicines, and how to ask for them:

Morning-After Pill: *Pastilla del dia despues.*

Yeast Infection: *Diflucan* (prescription). Saying "Monistat" usually does the trick.

Bacterial Infection: We're not sure of the official name, but the translation for this one is *infeccion bacterial.*

Rehydration Medicine: *Medicina para la rehydracion.*

Anti-nausea/Seasick medicine: *Pastillas en contra de la nausea y vomito.*

BED BUGS

Bed bugs are an issue in hostels all over the world. If and when the cluster of red bumps appears, usually on your extremities, the best thing to do is ignore it. Scratching the bites just causes irritation and then small red dots turn into gross puffy hives and maybe even scars. *No bueno.* If you can find some after-bite wipes, this will help with the itchiness so you are less tempted to scratch. You can check the seams of your mattress to spot the little buggers. Remember; there is no need to freak out. The bites are usually nothing more than unnerving (and a little embarrassing for some reason.)

TIP: If you're traveling to the north of Argentina where elevations are higher, bed bugs will not follow you as they cannot live in areas of high altitude.

Q&A
MEET AN OBGYN

GISELLE CARINO
Deputy Director of Programs, International Planned
Parenthood Federation/Western Hemisphere Region
Based Out Of: New York, NY

Giselle Carino works for IPPFW/HR, which provides family
planning to residents in Argentina. Here, she shares vital
information every woman should know before visiting Argentina.

**GGG: What sorts of female health issues do you think female
travelers should be aware of while in country?**

*The health issues for female travelers in Argentina are similar to
those in most other countries. While Argentina is a relatively safe
country, crime (including rape and sexual violence) does occur.
It's important for female travelers to take the usual precautions,
particularly when traveling alone.*

**GGG: In a country where terminating a pregnancy is illegal,
what options do women have?**

It is important to note that Argentinean law allows for the termination of pregnancy under specific circumstances, including rape and health reasons. While legal abortion services are not widely available, advocates and medical professionals have been working diligently in the last few years to increase access to safe and legal services in public hospitals.

In July 2009, a group of activists launched the Safe Abortion Hotline, www.womenonwaves.org/set-2023-en.html, which provides counseling and information to women seeking to terminate pregnancies. The telephone number to reach them is: 11156-664-7070.

FUSA, an affiliate of the International Planned Parenthood Federation, offers comprehensive sexual and reproductive health services for young people through the adolescent clinic at the Hospital Argerich in La Boca, Buenos Aires. These services include counseling on unwanted pregnancy and information to prevent unsafe abortions.

GGG: Is contraception widely available?

Contraception is widely available throughout Argentina. Contraceptive methods can be found in almost all pharmacies and can be purchased without a prescription. The government also provides family planning services free of charge to users of the public health system. However, government health centers often experience a shortage of supplies, providers who refuse to provide certain services on the grounds of "conscientious objection" and other barriers that limit women's access.

GGG: Are there women's clinics within Argentina? How should women find a gynecologist should they need one?

There are many different clinics and independent providers within Argentina. For more information on finding a clinician, please contact: FUSA: Fusa2000@gmail.com

The Ministry of Health free hotline from anywhere in the country is a good place both to have questions answered and find public center providers: 0800-222-3444 For more info visit: www.msal.gov.ar/saludsexual

Q&A
COSMETIC TOURISM

DR. SILVINA MONPELAT
Plastic Surgeon, Monpelat Estetica Medica Cirugia Plastica
(Clinica Monpelat)

www.monpelatsite.com.ar

It's no secret—Argentina is becoming increasingly known for cosmetic surgery, with nearly 1 in 30 going under the knife, according to nationwide statistics. It's so common, in fact, that you'll likely see men and women walking around Buenos Aires with post-op bandages.

Why is it so common? Argentina is home to some of the world's top surgeons, and the cost of surgery is about half of what you would pay in the western world. There are risks, however, and few options for legal repercussions if things go wrong.

We talked with Doctor Silvina Monpelat about this rising trend, what it means for Argentina and how visitors can minimize their risks.

GGG: Can you tell us more about cosmetic tourism in Buenos Aires? Is it a growing trend?

It has really been the fashion for the last 10 years. What happens with extranjeros (foreigners) is that it is more convenient for them to come here; it isn't just a question of cost—it is much, much cheaper here—but also that quality of surgery here in Argentina is very good. For approximately the last 15 years, Brazil and Argentina have provided exceptional medical care.

Plastic surgery is also an indicator of how the economy in Argentina is doing—when we are doing well, we have a lot of national clients. When the economy is doing poorly, foreigners flock here because of the exchange rate.

GGG: What is the process like for foreigners visiting for plastic surgery?

I have been working with extranjeros for a long time, and our only requirement is that people who come for surgery are here for at least 10–15 days so that we can ensure their recovery goes well. They don't have to be bed-ridden the whole time. They can go see tango shows, or walk around Palermo—we just don't recommend they take tango lessons or go skiing, etc.

We begin with an online consultation, and then request blood and heart tests from the individual's doctor. From there we can move forward with scheduling the surgery. When they arrive, we have another consultation, the surgery and follow-up. We work with a hotel, located immediately in back of our office, so that those having surgery can rent an apartment or room nearby. I work a lot with people from Spain, who return regularly for things like peels and laser removal (medicina asthetica). It is also very common for people who had surgery in the past to return to check on the first, and also to have another. For a lot of people, the price that they would pay for plastic surgery in the U.S. is the same as paying for both the ticket here and the surgery, and they get a vacation as well.

GGG: What are your top three recommendations for someone considering plastic surgery here?

1) Be sure to read online reviews of the medic you are considering, and if possible talk to past clients.

2) Have at least two doctors in the U.S. give a consultation in advance, and have the appropriate tests.

3) Request proof/confirmation of the surgeon's degrees/qualifications.

GGG: What are the risks?

As with any surgery, there are risks related to the patient's health. The most common are, as in any surgery, allergies to a medicine. In order to best address these risks, we operate with a team of nine people ranging from surgeons and nurses to cardiologists and psychologists. But in this office, at least, we have never had any complications resulting in a medical emergency.

GGG: What are the most popular surgeries performed on foreigners?

All of them, but the most frequent are surgeries of the face (lifts, Botox, etc.) and breast implants.

GGG: What is the age demographic that you serve, and what do they request?

The age range is enormous, and the overwhelming majority are women. There are many men who come, but the majority come for hair implants and peels, etc. The youngest women who come are 15–16, and usually they do leg and stomach tucks, removal of cellulite and breast implants, and the women of 93 years old have face-lifts. I have one client who has had 15 facelifts.

GGG: When people come to you, do they usually have an idea of what they want, or do they come and just sort of ask you to make them look better?

Ninety percent of the patients who come to us come with this idea, especially with facial surgery. With operations on the body, people usually know what they want. However, when it comes to surgeries of the face, people often ask. This is why we have a psychologist, to talk with the person and find out if what they want comes from someone else or from themselves, and to guide them through the process. After that, I talk with both, and then present a range of options and ideas to the client.

BEFORE YOU GO

Between wine, steak, mountain villages and pristine beaches, Argentina has got it all. These are just the things you really shouldn't miss.

Best Mountain Village: El Bolson
This little village nestled into the Andes between Bariloche and Esquel is truly magical—just ask anyone who has ever been. Better yet, go hang out by the river and climb the peaks and wander through forests littered with sculptures by local artists and decide for yourself.

Best Artisanal Craft Fair: Tilcara
Tilcara has a really awesome craft fair where you can find handmade goods, leather, jewelry and souvenirs.

Best Cheap Street Food: Salta
This one was really tough, but Salta, with its plethora of street vendors surrounding 9 de Julio, won our award for yummy cheap street food. Mendoza and its night markets was a close second.

Best Wine: Cafayate
Mendoza generally gets the buzz for good wine, but Cafayate gets our vote for producing the same quality wine for slightly less.

Best Antique Shopping: Mercado de Pulgas in Buenos Aires

This giant warehouse packed full of antique shops offers hours of wandering and a million opportunities for brilliant finds ranging from furniture and cameras to jewelry and 50+ year old *bombillas* (*mate* straws). The neighborhood surrounding the market is packed with little hole-in-the-wall shops as well.

Best Trekking: El Chalten

For variety of both levels and vistas, Chalten is the top pick for trekking adventures.

Best Cheap Accommodation: Córdoba

We love Córdoba. The funky city is much more relaxed than its big sister, Buenos Aires, and there are so many awesome, affordable accommodation options.

MONEY AND ATMS

Argentina Currency: Peso

The Argentina peso (AR$) comes in notes of 100, 50, 20, 10, 5 and 2 pesos; coins in 1 peso, 50, 25, 10 and 5 centavos. The $ sign is used to denominate Argentina pesos (notice it only has one line going through it). The current exchange rate as of June 2011 is AR$4.38: US$1.00. Always check the current exchange rate before you head somewhere new at websites like *www.xe.com or www.x-rates.com*.

ATMs and large banks can be found throughout the larger areas of Argentina, but all will charge you a conversion fee, and your bank will charge you various fees each time you withdraw as well.

The best exchange rate is offered at the large banks downtown, namely Metropolitana. The airport exchange rate will be significantly worse than elsewhere in the country, so change only a small amount to get you to your destination. Remember that you will be asked to provide your passport when exchanging currency.

TIPS ON MAKING YOUR PESOS LAST

- There is a scarcity of small bills and coins in Buenos Aires, which can make things difficult. Cashing a 100-peso bill can prove impossible in taxis and small grocery stores, but the bill can usually be cashed out in banks and large supermarkets. Keep this in mind when withdrawing pesos from an ATM and take out 90 or 190 rather than 100 or 200, that way you don't get all your money in hundred peso bills.

- New Argentine exchange regulations restrict purchasing dollars and taking dollars out of the country, which results in banks and exchange houses refusing to buy back Argentine pesos.

- No pesos? Carrying a small amount of USD can come in handy, as most restaurants, clothing stores and grocery stores will take U.S. currency at a reasonable rate. You may lose a little on the exchange, but it is well worth the convenience.

- Along those lines, U.S. dollars are the preferred foreign currency. Chilean and Uruguayan pesos can be readily exchanged at the borders, and U.S. dollars and Euros can be changed at exchange houses (*cambios*) in larger cities, but other currencies can be difficult to change outside Buenos Aires.

- If you have a savings and a checking account that are linked via online banking, bring debit or credit cards for each account. Go out with only one at time and keep the other in a safe place.

HOW TO PROTECT YOUR MONEY

Going out? We recommend carrying small pesos, ATM cards, and some U.S. cash with you. Keep your cards separated so you don't have everything in one place if it gets stolen, and always keep a cash reserve hidden somewhere, like in tampon boxes, bras and boots.

These days, traveler's checks are practically a thing of the past. They can be difficult to exchange in anything but large banks, coincidentally, where you'll get the worst rate.

Accommodation options in Argentina range from small guest-houses to 5-star hotels. Hostels generally prove to be the most affordable option, but prices fluctuate wildly. That being said, in some of the smaller towns it is worth comparing prices between hostels and small hotels or *hosterías*. Most hostels are able to provide information about your stay, and staff can help you arrange accommodation in your next destination. We scoured the country to help you find the best for your buck—the hostels, hotels and hosterías listed in this guidebook are all safe, convenient, clean and staffed with friendly faces.

Looking to stay a little longer?

HOW TO RENT AN APARTMENT IN BUENOS AIRES

If your two-week holiday just wasn't enough, you might be thinking of renting an apartment and staying a while. Buenos Aires is home to an increasingly large number of expats, and as such, the rental market has exploded. There are hundreds of apartments for rent in B.A. and just as many rental agencies, which can make things a bit confusing. Don't worry!

Whether you're looking for a place to chill out for two weeks, or want to make a more permanent move to Argentina, here is some information on renting an apartment in B.A.

Find Your Apartment
You can either rent an apartment through an agency or directly with a landlord. Agency listings are in every newspaper and magazine throughout the city. Apartments here will be all across the board in terms of price, location, and quality, so you're just going to have to do a little hunting. Many people also find their apartments on Craigslist.

If You Can't Speak Spanish...
Learn some. It will help you get off to a good foot with your landlord or agency and may even help bring down the price.

Don't Rent it Without Seeing It
And make sure that while you're seeing it, you're taking pictures of things and noting any damage found in the place. If your landlord is there watching you take pictures, even better.

Read Your Contract Closely
If it's in Spanish and you can't read it, ask for a copy in English. Be sure you know what you're signing before you pay a deposit.

Try to Pay in Pesos
With the market catering so heavily to U.S. and European travelers, most landlords in BA will want you to pay in dollars, which may be difficult and more expensive. It's a long shot, but if you can pay in pesos, you may save yourself a lot of time and hassle.

Don't Leave Without Your Deposit
If you've been a good tenant and have kept the place tidy and worked with your landlord in case of any damage, you're entitled to your deposit. Don't leave Buenos Aires without it! If your plane leaves at 5 p.m., tell your landlord it leaves at noon. Seriously.

Living in Argentina is an awesome way to get to know the city better. Happy hunting!

BARE BONES BUDGET

Argentina can be affordable if you navigate it as the locals do—travel by bus, eat on the street, and sleep in hostels or couch-surf. That being said, compared to travel in the rest of South America—other than Brazil—it is quite expensive. To live comfortably, you'll need a daily budget of roughly 80–120 pesos/day.

Meals on the street and in small restaurants will cost anywhere between 15 and 40 pesos. Budget accommodation will cost anywhere from 50–100 pesos, and transportation can range anywhere from 20 pesos (within a city) to 600 pesos from one city to the next. Keep in mind also that traveling around the north of Argentina is significantly less expensive than traveling around Patagonia.

Daily Budget: 100 pesos
You're Sitting Pretty With: 300 pesos

CELL PHONES

It's a good idea to get a cell phone to use in Argentina, and it is a relatively inexpensive investment. You can purchase a cell phone at just about any electronic store—the cheapest run about 200 pesos. Movistar and Claro are the most popular brands, and you can "recharge" by purchasing cards at most kiosks. Sometimes the store clerk will load the time for you automatically via a computer. Both systems seem to work fine; just be sure you receive a text message confirming that you've purchased credit before leaving the kiosk.

Don't want to give up your home phone number? Most plans can be put on hold at home for around $10 a month. Call your cell phone provider for details.

To call an Argentine phone number from another country, dial: +011 – 54 – 11 + area code + phone number.

ARGENTINA PUBLIC HOLIDAYS

Public holidays in Argentina can make traveling and finding accommodation a bit difficult, as Argentines love to travel on their three-day weekends. Keep this in mind and book in advance. For the most part, public transportation keeps a fairly regular schedule, but many shops and banks close, so do your grocery shopping in advance.

January 1: New Year's Day

March 24: Day of Remembrance for Truth and Justice

April 02: Day of the Veterans and Fallen of the Malvinas War

April 06: Good Friday

May 01: Labor Day

May 25: National Day (Anniversary of the 1810 Revolution)

June 18: National Flag Day

July 09: Independence Day

August 17: San Martín Day (Anniversary of the Death of General Jose de San Martín)

October 12: Day of Respect for Cultural Diversity

December 08: Virgin Mary's Immaculate Conception Day

December 25: Christmas Day

TANGO IN ARGENTINA

Maybe you saw "Scent of a Woman," maybe you heard about it because you're coming here, maybe you're a tango enthusiast who has danced all your life—whatever your background, the tango is an important part of Argentina's culture.

The tango started in the slums of Buenos Aires in the late 1800s/early 1900s. There are a number of theories about how and why the tango is, but one of our favorites is that when the gauchos would visit the clubs they would still be wearing their smelly, stiff chaps from riding horses. In order to avoid the stench, girls would keep their faces turned and tilted slightly upward, and hold their right hand low, near the gaucho's pocket, suggesting that he ought to pay her for her hospitality.

It is less and less common for the youth to take much interest, and very few people go out to dance the tango any more. Tango shows are still relatively common, although in some places they appear more and more aimed at tourists.

Best place to take tango lessons: We took lessons from Tango Piola. They were fun and affordable and conveniently located in Palermo Hollywood, with excellent and non-intimidating instructors. *www.tangopiola.com*

Best blog for learning more about the tango:
www.tangoinhereyes.blogspot.com.ar

Best place to see tango: *www.lacatedralclub.com*

Favorite tango song: *Por una cabeza* (1935) – music by Carlos Gardel, lyrics by Alfredo Le Pera

CORDS & WIRES

Electricity in Argentina is supplied through 230/240 volts, 50 hertz. For most electronics, an adapter/converter is necessary, unless the item has a multi-voltage option. Adapters can be found in most major grocery stores and in many small markets. Argentina power outlets accept rounded 2-pin and diagonal 2-pin plugs.

Video Format: PAL

Camera/Tech Repair is best found in Buenos Aires, Salta, Rosario or Ushuaia.

Internet is widely available—though you won't be able to get your dose of reality TV with Hulu or Netflix due to licensing issues.

WHEN TO GO

December–April
This is Argentina's summer. It's a great time to visit Patagonia as Buenos Aires and northern Argentina heats up, but it's also Argentina's high season, so things may get a little more expensive.

May–August
This is Argentina's winter, and it can get very cold. If you're hoping to ski, visit Bariloche and Ushuaia down in Patagonia.

The off-season months can bring spectacular weather. For whale watching, visit Puerto Madryn in September, and for incredible fall colors, visit Argentina in April or May.

PACKING LIST

Remember, you can purchase most everything you need in Argentina—except hot sauce, peanut butter and maple syrup. However, clothes are about on par with prices in the U.S. and electronics are extremely expensive!

This list is season and location dependent, but a good bare bones starting point:

- 3 light t-shirts (cotton, quick to dry)
- 3 tank tops
- 1 pair of shorts
- 2 pair of pants
- 1 pair of yoga pants
- 2 long-sleeve shirts
- 1 jacket
- 3–5 pairs of socks
- 1 pair of sleeping clothes
- 10–20 pairs of underwear (you can never have enough)
- 2 loose-fitting dresses or skirts
- Flip-flops
- Hiking boots
- 1 hat
- 1 pair of gloves
- 1 scarf
- 1 swimsuit
- Electrical adapters/chargers/batteries (electronics are expensive and hard to find)
- 1 pair of heels (especially important for tango lessons in Buenos Aires)
- Hot sauce (if you're into that)

Our theory is this: You can wear shirts and pants often before you have to wash them, but nothing feels as good as clean underwear. Bring a ton of underwear.

Hands down, the best travel companion in Argentina is the wine key. You never know when you'll need to pop open a bottle of Malbec. Bringing a scarf is also a good idea, especially one that's pretty enough to dress things up, that you can use as a towel in a bind, and large enough to operate as a blanket or shoulder wrap on buses when you need a little something extra.

Things to leave behind:

Purses
You'll have fun shopping for a relatively cheap and awesome leather purse or knit bag from Bolivia.

Cosmetics
From base layers to make-up remover, you can find anything you need here for about the same price as in the U.S.

SMOKING IN ARGENTINA

As a general rule of thumb, smoking is banned in most restaurants, bars and clubs. But, we use the word banned loosely. Some establishments allow it, and almost all have both inside and outside sections where it is allowed. If you see an ashtray or other people smoking, it's probably pretty safe to assume you can smoke, but to be polite, ask a waiter, bartender or employee, "¿Puedo fumar?" if you smoke.

GETTING AROUND

Air
Domestic flights run from Buenos Aires to most major hubs in both northern and southern Argentina. Flights come highly recommended for those trying to make their way to Ushuaia or El Calafate to avoid really, really long bus rides. The major companies are LAN, LADE and Aerolinas Argentinas.

Buenos Aires airport code: EZE

Bus
Buses run the length of Argentina and are reasonably priced and uncharacteristically comfortable. You can expect food, bathrooms and reclining seats on most bus lines. Book long bus tickets at the bus station, or buy your ticket directly on the bus for shorter rides. Some of our favorite companies are Via Bariloche, Andesmar and Chevallier.

Taxi
Private taxis are available in just about all large cities, especially in Buenos Aires. If you're traveling through Buenos Aires, be sure

to stick to Radio Taxis (black on bottom, yellow on top) because they are registered and metered.

Train

Trains extend north into the greater reaches of Buenos Aires and east as far as Mar de Plata. There are six main routes branching out of Buenos Aires that lead to Rosario, Rojas, Santa Rosa, Mar de Plata, Las Flores and Bahia Blanca. Train prices are very economical, but do generally take more time than bus travel. We recommend buying train tickets 3–14 days in advance.

ARGENTINA PROVINCES AND THEIR CAPITALS

Argentina is divided into 23 provinces and one federal district (Buenos Aires).

PROVINCE	CAPITAL
Buenos Aires	La Plata
Catamarca	San Fernando del Valle de Catamaraca
Chaco	Resistencia
Chubut	Rawson
Ciudad de Buenos Aires	Buenos Aires
Córdoba	Córdoba
Corrientes	Corrientes
Entre Ríos	Paraná
Formosa	Formosa
Jujuy	Jujuy
La Pampa	Santa Rosa
La Rioja	La Rioja
Mendoza	Mendoza
Misiones	Posadas
Neuquén	Neuquén
Río Negro	Viedma
Salta	Salta
San Juan	San Juan
San Luis	San Luis
Santa Cruz	Río Gallegos
Santa Fe	Santa Fe
Santiago del Estero	Santiago del Estero
Tierra del Fuego	Ushuaia
Tucumán	Tucumán

VISAS

Nationals of the United States, Canada, most western European countries, Australia, and New Zealand do not need visas to visit Argentina for less than 90 days.

As of 20 December 2009, U.S. citizens flying into Ezeiza International Airport must pay an entry fee of $140 USD. This fee is valid for 10 years and allows for multiple visits to the country.

In theory, upon arrival all non-visa visitors must obtain a free tourist card, good for 90 days and renewable for 90 more. In practice, immigration officials issue these only at major border crossings, such as airports and on the ferries and hydrofoils between Buenos Aires and Uruguay. Although you should not throw your card away, losing it is no major catastrophe; at most exit points, immigration officials will provide immediate replacement for free.

Make sure to check that your passport has at least six months' validity before traveling and that you have blank pages for visas as most take up entire pages.

If you're traveling around South America, bring with you two passport-sized photos should you need to show it to obtain additional visas.

BORDERS

Argentina is bordered by Chile, Bolivia, Paraguay, Brazil and Uruguay.

Is it Safe to Cross the Border?

Generally speaking, yes. Argentina has good relationships with the bordering countries, and most border crossings are straightforward as long as your documents are in order. Reports of scams involving local characters offering to "help" and then robbing tourists are most common on the border with Bolivia, but can happen anywhere. Your best bet is to travel during the day, and be alert. You should also speak enough Spanish or travel with someone that does so you can easily navigate the crossing. Changing money on the border always has its risks, so do what you can to change in advance.

For up-to-date information on all of the borders, visit:
www.gendarmeria.gov.ar

···················· FESTIVALS IN ARGENTINA ····················

January—Gualeguaychu Carnival de Pais
During Argentina's version of Carnival, large samba clubs compete for titles and honor through elaborate parades. The event takes place in Gualeguaychu, on Saturdays in January and February. It's three hours away from Buenos Aires by bus, and you can take a direct bus from the Retiro station in Buenos Aires.

March—Tilcara Carnival Festival
This festival is an opportunity for villagers of Tilcara to thank the earth for all it has given. It is believed that the devil possesses the souls of people during Carnival and it is at this time that the normally shy people of northern Argentina come to life. The festival lasts for nine days and ends with nine offerings to the earth, one for each day of the festivities. The devil is then put back in his hole and covered with rocks until the next year.

May—Arte Buenos Aires, Contemporary Art Fair
The fair marks the beginning of the cultural season in the Argentine capital. Visitors will find an exhibition designed to bring high-quality art to the public.

June—Festival Ciudad Emergente
More than 130,000 visitors flock to El Centro Cultural in the Recoleta neighborhood of Buenos Aires for this cultural event hosting art from young and upcoming artists in every genre ranging from graffiti and animation to poetry, film, fashion and design. Best part: It lasts five days. Even better part: It's free!
www.ciudademergente.gov.ar

August—Buenos Aires World Tango Festival
If there's anything that is quintessentially Buenos Aires, it's tango. That's why, for 18 days in August, B.A. residents and internationally-acclaimed dancers come out to celebrate through dancing competitions, displays, exhibitions, classes and film during the Buenos Aires World Tango Festival. Best of all, many of the events are free.

September—Semana Musical Llao Llao

Held in Bariloche, this event is a celebration of the art of classical music. Concerts are held throughout the town, while musicians from all around the world arrive in Bariloche to give solo and ensemble performances.

October—National Beer Festival

It's Argentina's version of Oktoberfest, and if you like beer, it's a heck of a good time. The event draws thousands to the provinces of Córdoba during two consecutive weekends in October, all celebrating—you guessed it—beer!

November—Buenos Aires Gay Pride Festival

Buenos Aires is home to a large gay community and thousands come out to show their support during the parade as part of the annual Buenos Aires Gay Pride Festival in November.

EVITA

Widely considered the most famous woman in Argentina's history, Evita is memorialized throughout Buenos Aires. She was both beloved and despised in her time, and it is said that on the day her death was announced, the streets filled with the country's poor and disenfranchised, weeping for their loss, and that behind closed doors, the wealthy popped bottles of champagne in celebration of her end.

You can find out more at the Eva Perón Museum in Palermo.

2988 Lafinur Street
+54 114-807-0306
www.evitaperon.org

GET INSPIRED WITH FILMS AND BOOKS

FILMS

"El Secreto de Sus Ojos" (2009 – Argentina)
(The Secret in Their Eyes)
An Argentine favorite, this movie chronicles the struggles of a legal counselor as he writes a novel detailing one of his past unresolved homicide cases involving a brutal rape. At the time of its release in 2009, it was the most viewed movie in Argentina since 1983.

"Nueve Reinas" (2000) (2000 – Argentina) (Nine Queens)
A con film involving rare stamps, tricky negotiations and suspicious characters complicate the plot and at the climax of the film, it's tricky to know who is conning whom.

"The Motorcycle Diaries" (2004)
Based on a journal written by Che Guevara in his early twenties, this film chronicles his adventures across Argentina, Chile, Peru, Columbia and Venezuela and his medical residency in a leper colony. The film highlights the evolution of Che's relationship with his friend, Alberto, throughout their journey. The film boasts a great soundtrack and some incredible cinematography. Che Guevara is from Rosario, Argentina—and if you're there, you can't help but see the signs pointing you to the home he lived in while he was there.

"Evita" (1996)
This adaptation of the Broadway musical depicts the infamous real-life story of Eva "Evita" Duarte de Perón, a young actress who rose from poverty to become the wife of then President Juan Perón. The story is one of love and politics, of class struggle and fear, and celebrates the life of the most famous woman in Argentine history—both beloved and despised in her time.

BOOKS

"In Patagonia" by Bruce Chatwin (1977)

"A Lexicon of Terror: Argentina and Legacies of Torture" by Marguerite Feitlowit (1999)

"Che Boludo: A Gringo's guide to Understanding the Argentines" by James Bracken (2007)

MORE INFORMATION

For more info, check out these awesome Argentina-inspired travel blogs:

www.travellerspoint.com
www.theargentinagringo.com

Q&A
FASHION IN ARGENTINA:
AN INTERVIEW WITH A FASHION DESIGNER

VERONICA OBRADOR ESPINA, 26

Veronica Obrador Espina is a fashion designer for Vans in Argentina. Originally from just outside the city, she is studying fashion design at the University of Buenos Aires, and has been working in fashion design for the last six years.

Excited about new trends in Buenos Aires, especially amongst young, up-and-coming designers, Vero agreed to give us BAs fashion 101.

GGG: Where do you work and what do you do?

For the last nine months I've been a fashion designer at Vans, and for five years before that I worked with a local designer. I studied (and am still studying) fashion design at the University of Buenos Aires (UBA).

GGG: Tell us about the latest fashion trends in Buenos Aires.

One of the biggest changes in fashion in Argentina is that we used to follow the trends of European fashion very closely and we're moving away from that. Right now, it's much more of a culture of "everything goes" or "vale todo" and fashion bloggers play a big role in how fashion is shaped here. And, there is a huge climb in the number of young designers contributing to the fashion world. Markets like Plaza Serrano in Palermo create a space for young and up-coming designers to show and sell their designs on the weekends without having to pay the rent (which is very high) for a place all week long.

The trend right now is marked by lots of colors, mixed patterns and textures, giant purses and platform shoes. Fluos (florescent) are really in right now, and are going to be even more popular come summer time. We've come a long way from the idea of "your belt has to match your purse," etc. Now, it's more in style to make sure nothing matches. Additionally, in Argentina, the styles are complemented by a very natural look on the faces of the women. The "in" style is to wear minimal make-up (clean face), with long hair that hasn't had much or anything done to it, down or in a high bun.

Oh, and lots of really colorful bracelets, and detailed and colorful nails are popular as well!

GGG: What do you recommend that women visiting Argentina bring with them?

As little as possible and buy it here!

GGG: What things should women visiting Argentina buy here?

The best thing to buy here is definitely leather: bags, boots, coats—all of it! Shoes in general are good to buy here because they're really unique and fun. Scarves and leggings are also really popular and they easy to find, both for cheap and of really high quality and design.

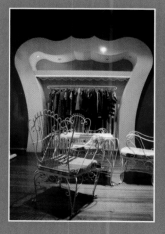

CULTURE & CUSTOMS

Friendliness, curiosity and respect will get you a long way as an *extranjera*, or foreigner. The best way to get off on the right foot with Argentines is to speak some Spanish—most people consider it rude to visit a country and not know at least the basics.

FAMILY AND RELIGION

The majority of Argentines who identify with a specific religion are Roman Catholic, and Catholicism is the official religion of the state, although the constitution guarantees religious freedom. More than 60 percent of Argentines self-identify as being spiritual, without relating to any one religion in particular. Three quarters of the population is said to never, or rarely, attend ceremonies of worship. And, while Sundays are definitely family days, they are not generally centered around a religious celebration or gathering.

GREETING

It's important to say hello to those you meet, usually with a single kiss on the cheek. Exchanging greetings to people you come in contact with is extremely important, and is a way to show respect. It is considered rude to not say hello, especially in small towns where everyone knows each other. Even when you are in a store or kiosk purchasing something, it is rude to start immediately with asking for what you want without first greeting the person behind the desk.

Some common phrases:

¿Hola, como estas? Hello, how are you?
Buenos dias. Good morning.
Buenos tardes. Good afternoon.
Buenas noches. Good night.
¿Como andas? How are things going?
¿Todo bien? Everything good?
¡Ciao, suerte! Goodbye and good luck.

HISTORY

Argentina is a mosaic of immigrant populations, meshed with a very small remaining indigenous population. Nearly 95 to 98 percent of Argentines are of European decent, the overwhelming majority from Spain, Italy and Germany, and the country has a very European feel, from language and customs to architecture and industry. The indigenous make up only 1–4 percent of the population, and are highly marginalized and often overlooked, specifically when it comes to land and resource rights.

Before the arrival of the Spanish in 1536, Argentina was inhabited by a number of nomadic tribes: the Mapuche, Tehuelche and Yamana of Patagonia and Tierra del Fuego, and the Guarani who primarily inhabited the tropical northeast, just to name a few. Conflicts with indigenous tribes held Spanish conquistadors at bay for about another 30 years before they returned and founded Buenos Aires in 1587.

Colonialist development remained isolated to the BA region until nearly 300 years later, when then-President Nicolás Avellaneda embarked on a campaign of extermination to open up Patagonia for settlement and sheep rearing.

In Buenos Aires, industry grew rapidly and wealth consolidated in the hands of those controlling the ports (hence the nickname *porteño* for Argentines originally from BA). Mass migration from rural areas to the city only widened the gap, until Colonel Juan Domingo Perón came to power in 1946. Famous for his social welfare and economic programs that eased the pressure on the working class, Perón and his second wife, Evita, would become two of the most popular figures in Argentine history. Although celebrated for his social programs, Perón's reputation was stained with reports of abuse of power by means of squashing free press and political debate. Ousted to Spain for 18 years, Perón returned to power in 1973, and power was turned over to his third wife, Isabel Martinez de Perón, after his death in 1974. She gained control of a nation on the brink of economic and political collapse. In 1976 a military junta seized power and imposed martial law, thus beginning what would later be known as The Dirty War. The junta has since been charged with 2,300 political murders, more than 10,000 political arrests and the disappearance/murder of 20,000–30,000 people.

A series of leaders took the stage before Raúl Alfonsín was elected in 1983, and succeeded in getting the country back on track by curbing inflation, settling various territorial disputes, and trying military officers for crimes committed during The Dirty War. However, Alfonsín and his successors would continue to struggle with grave economic troubles until everything came to a head with an economic crash in 2001.

Unemployment hit 18.3 percent and Argentines took to the streets on strike and in protest. In January 2002, Argentina defaulted on $140 billion in foreign debt—the biggest default in world history—and sent potential foreign investors running. Commonly referred to in Argentina as "la crisis," this period is marked by civil unrest and widespread distrust of the government.

Néstor Kirchner became president in 2003, and began tackling the economic crisis. Through a series of reforms, Kirchner achieved a growth rate of nearly 8 percent, paid off Argentina's remaining debt, and began prosecuting perpetrators of The Dirty War. For these actions, Kirchner was re-elected and by the end of his second term in 2007 was considered one of Argentina's most popular presidents. By the end of his term, unemployment had fallen to just under 9 percent, and he has succeeded in steering the economy away from strict alignment with the U.S., working instead to grow relationships with Argentina's South American neighbors.

Kirchner's wife, Cristina Fernández de Kirchner, took over in 2007, becoming the first woman to be elected president in Argentina. Many of his policies would continue, but despite a rise in the level of optimism nationwide, poverty, unemployment and general insecurity remain serious issues for many middle and lower-class Argentine families.

LOS DESAPARECIDOS (THE DISAPPEARED) AND THE DIRTY WAR

Desaparecidos is a Spanish word that means "the disappeared." In Argentina, the term is used to refer to the victims of The Dirty War that lasted between 1976 and 1983, when thousands of Argentines were arrested and never seen or heard from again. The exact number of the disappeared remains disputed; recent estimates say that the terror claimed anywhere from 22,000 to 30,000 people.

On March 24, 1976, a military junta overthrew the Argentine government and established a new regime known as the National Reorganization Process. The new government quickly began a massive campaign to eliminate so-called "subversive terrorists." Under the regime's broad definition, dissidents and innocent civilians alike were swept up and sent to secret detention centers to be tortured and killed.

Most of the victims, in fact, had nothing to do with "subversive terrorism." They included journalists, nuns, priests, trade union leaders, students and doctors. Some victims were selected at random; others were arrested because they happened to be acquainted with dissidents. Many of the people arrested were pregnant women; after they gave birth in detention, their newborns were confiscated and given to military families to raise.

By 1983, public anger and unrest caused by the disappearances and an economic crisis was threatening the junta's hold on the government. In an effort to divert the public's attention and unify the country, the junta invaded and seized the disputed Falkland Islands. After British forces successfully expelled Argentina from the islands, the regime's power at home rapidly crumbled and democracy was restored in October 1983. It is believed that the junta destroyed the records of The Dirty War's victims shortly before its fall. To this day, most of the remains of the victims have never been recovered.

Today, the victims of The Dirty War are commemorated by the Day of Remembrance for Truth and Justice, an Argentine holiday celebrated on March 24, the anniversary of the 1976 coup. For more information, visit www.yendor.com/vanished, a website dedicated to recovering as much evidence as possible about the disappeared victims.

— *Justyn Dillingham*

CURRENT POLITICS

Argentina consists of 23 provinces plus a federal district, the city of Buenos Aires. The Argentine constitution establishes a republic under a representative and federal system, and three separate branches of government: executive, legislative, and judicial.

The executive branch is exercised by the President and Vice-president of the nation, elected for a four-year term, and who may be reelected for one additional term.

The legislative branch is bicameral and includes the Senate (composed of three senators from each province and from the city of Buenos Aires) and the House of Representatives (composed of representatives elected directly and in proportion to each district's population). The judicial branch is vested in the Supreme Court and lower courts of justice.

Each province has adopted its own constitution in accordance with the National Constitution, to rule its administration.

The current National Constitution dates from 1853 but was amended in 1860, 1898, 1957, and 1994. The last amendment was made in August 1994, and it allows the president's reelection for an additional term.

Argentina is currently a representative democracy, but has struggled with recurring economic and institutional crises that have plunged the country into military regimes and coup d'états a number of times since the 1930s.

Cristina Fernández de Kirchner, of the Justicialast party, is Argentina's current president, and the first woman to be elected president of Argentina. Her husband, Néstor Kirchner, was president before her, and her success is often attributed to his popularity. Cristina, commonly referred to by her first name, has been in power since 2007, and won reelection in 2011 with a 37 percent margin of victory.

Although poverty and unemployment have decreased over the last decade, rising inflation, estimated at around 25 percent, energy shortages, price controls and the withdrawal of foreign investment threaten their sustainability.

While local opinions about Cristina are mixed, there is a general mistrust for the government amongst most Argentines, specifically when it comes to issues of the economy and corruption.

CONFLICT OVER FALKLAND ISLANDS

It has been 30 years since the Falklands War in which Argentina invaded the Falkland Islands, located 240 nautical miles off the eastern coast of Argentina. The affiliation of the islands, referred to by the UK as the Falklands and by Argentines as Las Malvinas, has been disputed virtually since their discovery in the 16th century. In response to the Argentine invasion in 1982, the British sent fierce naval and air forces, and retook the islands just two months after Argentina launched their initial invasion. The war resulted in the deaths of 255 British and 649 Argentine soldiers, sailors and airmen, as well as three civilians. Despite what is considered a victory by the United Kingdom, Argentina continues to claim rights to the islands, and the 30-year anniversary on June 14, 2012, brought fresh emotion and resentment to the table.

President Cristina Fernandez de Kirchner made an appearance on the 30-year anniversary of the war, to the United Nations to continue arguing that the Falkland Islands are Argentine territory and should not be under British rule. At the same committee meeting, a representative from the Falkland Islands' Legislative Assembly told the committee that his people requested only the right to determine their own future, a right guaranteed them under the UN charter. The representative also cited a pole that found 96 percent of the islanders wish to keep British rule. While some Argentines vehemently support President Kirchner's efforts to reclaim the territories, others see it as a diversion tactic to distract from more serious issues (primarily economic) on the mainland.

CULTURAL SENSITIVITIES

The Argentines are generally pretty open and friendly people, and there aren't a lot of major no-no's, but here are a few pointers about cultural sensitivities to navigate cautiously in conversation.

Greetings
It is considered distant, cold and sometimes rude in Argentina if you don't kiss on the cheek when greeting someone new. For men this can be especially trying, and sometimes foreign women are put off by men who go in for the kiss right of the bat. Don't be alarmed—it's the custom and is usually performed both for greetings and when saying goodbye.

Las Malvinas
This all depends on who you talk to, but generally speaking it is still a sore subject for most Argentines. Some feel passionately about the subject but others, especially of the younger generations, wave their hand or signal in one way or another that they couldn't care less.

Politics
Much the same as Las Malvinas, and much the same as in any other place, some people feel very strongly about the president and politics while others seem to not care much either way. That being said, there seems to be a general consensus that the economy is in disarray, and has been for some time.

River Plate versus Boca Juniors
While Argentina has a ton of soccer teams, the two major teams are River Plate and Boca Juniors and you'll be hard-pressed to find someone who would cheer for both. There is a long history between the two—both gaining their start in La Boca neighborhood in the early 1900s. The story goes that River moved to the more affluent neighborhood and that its fan base changed accordingly. While both teams do have supporters from all social classes, there definitely seems to be a stronger support for Boca Juniors amongst the working class. Boca fans call River fans "*gallinas*," claiming their players are chickens while River fans call Boca fans "*chanchitos*" claiming their stadium smells of little pigs. Argentines support one or the other, even if they have another favorite team, and they're passionate about it. When River Plata or La Boca Juniors have a game, you'll know it by the yelling, hollering and pot-banging in the streets.

GAUCHOS OF ARGENTINA

Deemed the wanderers of the Pampas, *gaucho* refers to a population of cowboys in charge of the significant cattle trade in Argentina, known for their superior horsemanship. Marked also as rough, rambling, solo-traveling womanizers who carry only a *facon* (a large knife generally tucked into the rear of the gaucho's sash), gauchos are a trademark of Argentine culture. Portrayed often in Argentine literature and cinema as a symbol against corruption, gauchos fought and prevailed in the Argentine War of Independence against the Spanish monarchy.

Typical Gaucho Dress

- *Poncho* (used as saddle bags and sleeping gear)
- *Bombachas* (loose-fitting pants)
- *Tirador* or *chiripa* (piece of cloth fashioned much like a diaper and used to hold up the bombachas)
- The aforementioned *facon*

Gauchos are credited with the creation of two of Argentina's most common food and beverage: *asado* and *yerba mate* (the highly caffeinated tea-like drink sipped and shared amongst friends from a gourd).

Gauchos of Argentina

HOW TO DRINK MATE LIKE A LOCAL

Most famously known as a drink of the gaucho culture, *mate* has its roots in the highlands of Brazil, Paraguay and Argentina, where the small native tree grows. The dried leaves and stems of the tree are brewed and consumed by nearly 92 percent of households in Argentina. The drink contains 1 percent caffeine, and offers a buzz similar to that of coffee. It has a bitter taste that may take some getting used to, but drinking mate is a social activity that will introduce you to a number of locals. While mate is prepared in several different fashions, here is a basic guide to enjoying mate in Argentina.

Terms

Mate: This term refers to both the tea and the gourd (traditionally made from calabasha) from which it is served.

Yerba: Refers to the mixture of tea and herbs itself.

Bombilla: The name for the straw used for drinking mate. Traditionally made of silver, these straws fan out at the bottom with small holes or slits to allow liquid to pass through while blocking the herbs.

Mate cocida: The "tea bag" version of mate. This is generally considered an entirely different drink altogether, is generally drunk from a normal mug, and is not associated with gaucho culture.

Social Customs

Mate is generally enjoyed in a group, and the person who offers the mate will remain in charge of serving everyone while the drinks are enjoyed. The server will take the first mate, as it is generally the most bitter, and then will offer it to guests thereafter. If you are invited and agree to join a group for some mate, keep these things in mind:

- Once you say thank you, the assumption is that you do not want any more. So, only say thank you when you are mate-saturated.

- Do not touch the straw. While nothing awful will happen, it is just generally considered a bit rude.

- While you don't have to chug the mate, sitting with the mate for a prolonged period of time is frowned upon.

- Some say drinking cold mate can make you sick to your stomach, although some purposefully drink it cold during summer months. You might have to test this one out for yourself.

- Depending on where you are in the country and whom you are with, additional herbs, sugar, coffee, or even milk may be added to the yerba. Give them a try and decide what works best for you!

Step-by-step

1. Buy a mate gourd, thermos, bombilla and yerba. You should be able to buy all of this for less than 150 pesos.

2. Invite a group of people to join you for mate.

3. Heat the water. This is actually a bit tricky as boiling water kills the mate.

4. You'll want to heat the water until just after it begins simmering, and then pour it into your Thermos. (You can definitely just use the tea pot as well, but most people serve mate from a Thermos as it stays warm without have to reheat, etc.).

5. Fill the mate gourd approximately two-thirds full with yerba. Place the palm of your hand over the opening in the gourd

and shake. When you pull your hand away, you will have a light green dust on your palm. Blow it off and repeat process 2-3 times.

6. Tap the mate gourd slightly to settle the yerba, and tilt the gourd so that the mate inside is uneven.

7. Pour a tiny bit of water into the side with the least mate and wait about 20 seconds.

8. Firmly insert the bombilla into the place where you poured the water. Try not to move it around too much.

9. Fill the mate gourd to the brim with hot water. Take the first drink yourself as it will be the most bitter. Drink all of it, refill the gourd with hot water, and pass to the next person. It doesn't seem to matter too much if you pass to the left or right, but once you choose a direction, keep passing around the circle that same direction. When you pass someone the gourd, be sure to pass it to them with the bombilla facing their direction.

Enjoy!

SEX AND SEXUALITY

Relative to the U.S., Argentines are fairly open and progressive when it comes to sex and sexuality. Same-sex marriage has been legal since 2010, and the LGBT community in Buenos Aires is active and growing. In terms of dating and relationships –and it of course varies from individual to individual—by and large there is a fairly open and casual approach by the younger generations. What this means for you as a traveler or *extranjera*: communicate. If you decide to date an Argentine or are just looking for a fling, the best bet is to be clear about your expectations. If you plan on dating, monogamous relationships tend to be the exception here, not the rule, and you'll spare yourself some heartache in the long run if you don't assume.

There is also a pretty widespread assumption that if you ask a girl from the U.S. to sleep with you, she will— just keep that in mind when that cute boy from the bar is chatting you up.

POLICE

Argentine police have a reputation for excessive violence, with 8.7 percent of the population reporting some form of violence and abuse by the police in 2009—one of the worst rates in Latin America. It's a sensitive subject in Argentina, following the dictatorship, and something that Argentines generally have very strong opinions about. What this means for you, generally speaking, is that Argentine police are not especially quick to help you out in a bind.

They aren't necessarily going to make things worse for you (although there are reports of police asking for bribes), but as they are paid minimally they aren't especially inclined to help you out, and should you be faced with having to report something, bear down for a lengthy and probably frustrating process.

If you are driving around the country, particularly in the north, be sure to always carry all the necessary documentation, as there are an increasing number of police checkpoints where arbitrary tickets are given.

During and after the economic crisis in 2001, kidnappings by police of affluent businessmen were common, as were kidnappings of ordinary people for smaller ransoms.

Some things to know:

• The safest neighborhood in Buenos Aires is Puerto Madero, both because it is one of the wealthiest and because, being a port neighborhood, it is protected by the National Guard instead of the police.

• Argentines have very little trust for the military and police due to the widespread corruption, violence and disappearances during The Dirty War.

• Corruption within local police does happen and some officers may solicit bribes. If you get stuck and are ever asked for money, comply.

DRUGS

Marijuana (*marijuan*) is legal for personal use in Argentina, but cultivating, selling and transporting marijuana is prohibited. It is common to see people smoking marijuana on the sidewalks, but it is not common in bars or clubs. While Argentina does not suffer drug-related violence and struggles the same way that some countries in Latin America do, it is increasingly struggling with the trafficking of cocaine and other narcotics.

DID YOU KNOW?

- Per capita, Argentine women undergo the highest number of plastic surgeries in the world, and more than 30 percent of its women suffer from some form of eating disorder.

- Ninety-eight percent of Argentines can trace their roots to Europe, namely Spaniards and Italians.

- The national Argentinean sport is *pato*, which is a mix of basketball and polo. However, very few Argentines talk about or even play it—soccer is much more popular.

- Since the 16th century, Argentina has maintained its status as one of the largest producers of wine in the world, and boasts roughly 1,800 wineries.

- Likely a byproduct of strong Italian influence in the country, it has become customary for Argentines to eat *gnocchi* (potato dumplings called ñoquis in Argentina) on the 29th of each month. Made of potato, flour and salt, gnocchi was a cheap meal, ideal for the last days of the month when money was tight. For good luck, don't forget to place a couple dollars under the plate while you consume the gnocchi.

- Contrary to widespread belief, Ernesto "Che" Guevara was not Cuban but Argentine. He was born in the city of Rosario in 1928, and you can visit his childhood home in Alta Gracias, Córdoba.

- Argentines set the world record for beef consumption, taking in more than 60 kg. of beef per person each year.

BUENOS AIRES

With nearly 13 million residents, Buenos Aires, commonly referred to as BA and written as BsAs, holds rank as the second-largest metropolitan area in South America. Dubbed the "Paris of Latin America," the architecture of Buenos Aires is influenced heavily by the French, Italian and Spanish immigrants who have made it their home.

The neighborhoods are as diverse as the Argentines themselves and there's something for everyone, from the cobblestone streets of San Telmo to the bustling markets of Once, the quaint coffee shops in Palermo, and the historic Teatro Colón. The bustling city center boasts all the musts of a big city, from diverse food and drink to a plethora of museums, nightclubs and shopping opportunities.

We've divided BsAs into five of the most visited neighborhoods: Palermo, Belgrano, San Telmo, Recoleta and Retiro/El Centro, with a final section on additional hot spots. Each neighborhood includes a brief description, accommodation and specific sites.

Best Place to Shop:
Palermo

Best Place to See Tango:
San Telmo

Best Place to Sip Mate and People Watch:
El Centro

FIRST, FINDING YOUR BEARINGS

Depending on where you land, B.A. can feel really accessible or really overwhelming. We benefited greatly from establishing a comfort zone in Palermo before heading to the city center, where it can be easier to get thrown off course. Even in the center, everyone is friendly and it isn't too confusing. That being said, streets stop and start often, and you can't rely on street signs being present to get you where you need to be. The bus system seems very complicated at first. Pick up a *Guia T* (any tourist office will have one) and a good map of the city, and learn how to use this site: *www.mapa.buenosaires.gov.ar* and you will master Buenos Aires in no time.

SAFETY AND SECURITY

As with any other big city, carry as little as possible on you, guard your possessions, and keep your eyes peeled. Buenos Aires is not known for violent crime, but pickpocketing and robberies are common. Electronics are a major target for thieves, so limit your camera use in risky areas; we heard plenty of stories from travelers who were robbed at gun or knifepoint for their cameras (even little point-and-shoots). If you have to walk at night, try not to walk for long distances and don't go it alone. If you can, avoid areas like La Boca, Retiro and Once at night. If you ever feel unsafe, hop in a taxi—they're all over the city.

WATCH OUT

Near Retiro, there is an increasingly common act in which someone pours something gross onto your bag from above, much resembling bird poop. When you remove your bag to clean it off, two older women and a young man (generally) will offer to help, then take off running with your bag.

In general, if anything feels off or if someone rushes up to you and seems overly friendly, it is best to politely decline, hold onto your belongings, and carry on your way.

Traveling at night

Argentines eat and party late (it is not uncommon for dinner to start between 10 and 11 p.m.) and because of this, moving around at night is a must. Fortunately, public transport (*colectivos*) and taxis are available all night long. When going out at night, take only the minimum in your purse.

Always, always tuck an additional 100 pesos in a bra, sock, underwear, anywhere hidden really, but have it somewhere secret. For 100 pesos, you can catch a taxi to just about anywhere in the city, and that's the idea.

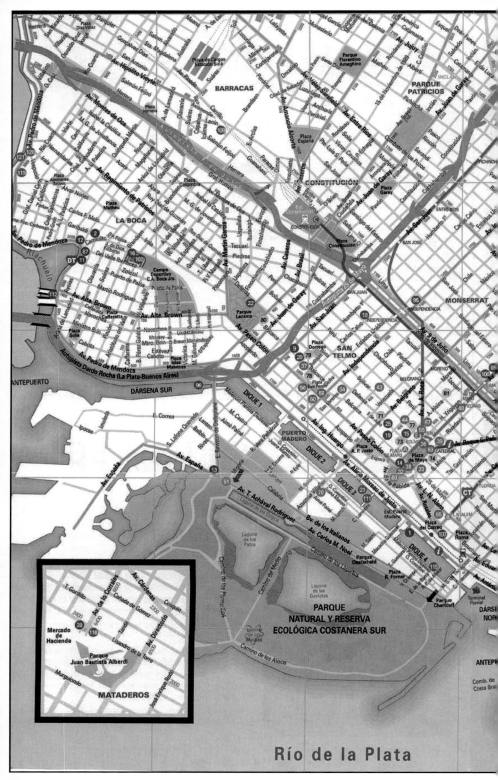

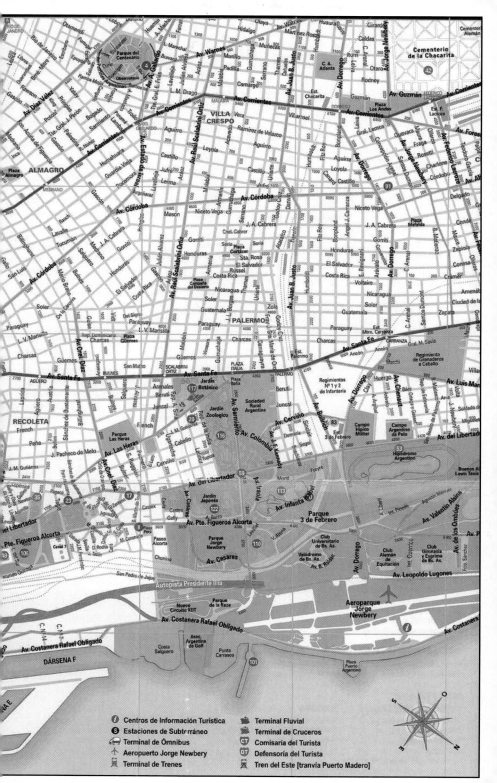

Centros de Información Turística

🛥 Terminal Fluvial

S Estaciones de Subterráneo

🚢 Terminal de Cruceros

🚌 Terminal de Ómnibus

GT Comisaría del Turista

✈ Aeropuerto Jorge Newbery

DT Defensoría del Turista

🚆 Terminal de Trenes

🚋 Tren del Este [tranvía Puerto Madero]

Colectivos/buses

These clearly marked, multi-colored buses have sitting and standing room and run 24 hours. They can be incredibly effective—*if* you have some patience and the time to use them. The routes can be a bit confusing, and you must have small change (*monedas*), or a pre-charged SUBE card to ride the bus. Colectivos are also the cheapest way to find your way around the city, and you can follow their routes in a *Guia T* or on their website. *www.mapa.buenosaires.gov.ar*

Subte

The *subte*, or subway, is one of the easiest ways to move about BsAs. It usually closes between 10 and 11 p.m., but during the day there is no easier way to bounce between neighborhoods. However, it doesn't reach far beyond the central part of the city and is occasionally closed because of strikes. You can buy more than one ticket a time, but be prepared for difficulty breaking large bills. *www.subte.com.ar*

Train

The main train system in Buenos Aires operates out of Retiro (the same place where the buses leave and arrive) in the center of the city. For navigating the suburbs of Buenos Aires, including Belgrano, San Isidro and Olivos, the train is very helpful and much faster than trying to use colectivos. It also closes between 10 and 11 p.m. It is very cheap—tickets usually cost 1–2 pesos.

Taxi

Private taxis are easy to find; we recommend sticking with Radio Taxis as they are registered and generally carry a good reputation.

Walking

If walking is your thing, you'll love Buenos Aires. Just be sure to take a map!

Transport from Ezeiza International Airport

To get to Buenos Aires from the airport, take a Radio Taxi for 150–170 pesos, or take the bus, which has several stops throughout Buenos Aires, for around 65 pesos. *www.tiendaleon.com.ar/home/home.asp*

BUENOS AIRES SUBWAY/METRO MAP

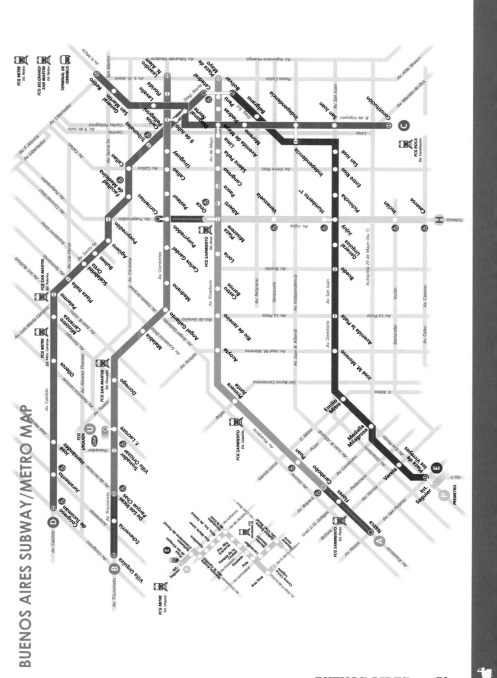

Buenos Aires Bike Tour
Whether you're visiting Barrio Chino, heading to the ecological reserve, or are taking in plazas and parks, biking is definitely one of the best ways to see the city. There are a number of companies who offer tours, but we highly recommend Biking Buenos Aires as they are reliable, knowledgeable, and fun. Tours run between 3-7 hours and generally start at around 200 pesos. The bikes are comfortable cruisers, and the company is very professional and great about making sure everyone is comfortable and safe. www.bikingbuenosaires.com

Graffiti Tour
If biking your way around the city just isn't your thing, www.graffitimundo.com offers great walking/mini-bus tours of the same amazing street art for about 100 pesos.

La Boca
One of Buenos Aires' most famous attractions, this popular tourist destination is becoming more and more of a tourist trap. The buildings, painted by Benito Quinquela Martín are beautiful and the neighborhood itself is interesting and older than most BA neighborhoods.

If you go, be sure to bring as little as you need and guard your valuables as robberies in the area are increasingly common.

The home of the famous Argentine artist, Benito Quinquela Martin, has been turned into a museum (8 pesos) where you can view the personal spaces that he once occupied and some of his most important pieces of work. The rooftop terraces where some of his sculptures are displayed, offer a great panoramic view of the city. While in the neighborhood, be sure to check out the stadium and museum of one of Argentina's most popular soccer teams, La Boca. You can arrive to La Boca by colectivo or private taxi. We recommend asking your hostel for details. There are also two companies that offer tours of La Boca, or include a stop in La Boca in a broader tour (starting around 200 pesos): www.buenostours.com.ar or www.bsas4u.com.

MALBA (Museo de Arte Latinoamericano de Buenos Aires)

This beautiful and modern museum opened in 2001, and has the Costantini Collection on permanent display. It also prides itself in being a dynamic cultural center with constantly revolving art, film and cultural exhibitions. It costs 25 pesos, unless you are a student in which case it is 12 pesos. Additionally, Wednesday's general admission is only 12 pesos. _www.malba.org.ar_

Puerto Madero

This neighborhood is the newest in Buenos Aires, boasting modern buildings and design, and is by far one of the most expensive places to live. Puerto Madero backs up to an ecological reserve, and is guarded by the navy instead of the police (making it the safest neighborhood in the city). If you're seeking fine dining and ritzy clubs, this is your spot. Otherwise, we recommend checking out the ecological reserve and then hitting one of the many tents on the boardwalk for some of the best _bondiola_ (grilled pork shoulder) sandwiches in town.

PALERMO

The largest neighborhood in Buenos Aires, Palermo is a relatively tranquil area with beautiful parks and tree-lined cobblestone streets as well as some of the city's best bars and restaurants. Palermo is broken down into three main parts: Palermo Hollywood—the trendiest area—Palermo Viejo, and Palermo SoHo. The U.S. Embassy and the Buenos Aires Zoo and Botanical Garden are located in Palermo.

THINGS TO DO

Mercado de Pulgas
This giant warehouse boasts loads and loads of antiques, and is open every day of the week from about 11 a.m. to 6 p.m., although it varies. It's busiest on the weekends, with most shop owners there on Saturday. If antiques are your thing, give yourself the better part of a day for wandering and tinkering.

Avenida Dorrego 1700 – Palermo

Bosques de Palermo
This urban forest, made up of more than 60 acres of protected park complete with lakes, rose gardens, sculptures, and green-ways, is a welcome escape from the bustling center.

Located between Libertador and Figueroa Alcorta Avuenes

Gecko Hostel

Nestled into a neat, open-air design with multiple rooftop hangouts, this hostel in Palermo Hollywood offers a great atmosphere for getting to know fellow travelers from all over. The staff is fun and super-helpful, and a number of students and expats live in the hostel's long-term residencia rooms, and have created a fun and active community there. There is a pool/ping-pong table, and most nights a crowd gathers in the hostel bar, which is set apart from the rest of the hostel, so if it's your night for catch-up sleep, you won't be bothered by the noise. Breakfast, although simple, is included in the price.

Cost: A traditional dorm with shared bathroom is 60 pesos, private single 130 pesos and a private double 180 pesos.

From Retiro, take Line C to the Diagonal Norte stop, and skip trains to Line D, all the way to Carranza. Pass under the bridge and walk two blocks on Santa Fe before turning right on Bonpland. Walk three blocks and the hostel will be halfway up the third block on the left. The sign is a bit hard to see, so keep your eyes peeled for a yellow building with green bars on the windows. Taxis from Retiro will run 25–30 pesos.

Bonpland 2233
+54 114-771-0910
gecko@geckohostel.com.ar
reservas@geckohostle.com.ar
www.geckohostel.com.ar

La Rocca

A great option for the price, La Rocca offers all the amenities in a clean and fun atmosphere, and a great location. Breakfast, free international and national phone calls, emergency medical assistance, and luggage storage are all included in the price. They have a fully stocked bar, ping-pong and foosball table as well. If you're looking into an extended stay in BsAs, La Rocca Properties has more than 500 apartments throughout the city and can be a great resource for getting something sorted for a longer stay.

Cost: Dorms with eight beds are 45 pesos/night, and prices go up from there to 200 pesos/night for a double bed with a private bathroom. If you plan on staying for a while, pay six days in advance and you get the seventh night for free. This hostel also has a monthly stay option for 900 pesos, which is very reasonable.

From Retiro, take subway line C to Diagonal Norte. Hope on line B and get off on Callao. Walk one block to the west on Callao and you will find the hostel on your left.

Avenida Callao 341
+54 114-372-8898
laroccacallao@gmail.com
www.laroccahostel.com

Eco Pampa Hostel
This is one of the few hostels that really puts an emphasis on minimizing their impact on the environment, with solar-powered lighting, recycled fixtures and antique furniture, low waste toilets, and more. Additionally, they have an awesome rooftop terrace, they're located in a great location in the middle of Palermo, and each room has

Wi-Fi access and a private bathroom. The dorms are sometimes mixed, but are usually gender-specific.

Cost: Prices range from 60 pesos for an eight-person dorm room to 400 pesos for a three-bed boutique.

From Retiro, take subway line D to Plaza Italia. Walk southeast four blocks on Jorge Luis Borges and take a left on Guatemala. The hostel will be on your right.

Guatemala 4778
+54 114-831-2435
ecoinfo@hostelpampa.com.ar
www.hostelpampa.com.ar

SHOPPING

Plaza Serrano
For the latest in Buenos Aires fashion, head to Plaza Serrano in Palermo every weekend for a gathering of the city's up-and-coming designers. The range of prices runs the gauntlet from cheap vendors from Bolivia to some of the most expensive designers in Buenos Aires, and the people-watching is spectacular.

Located at the intersection of Jorge Luis Borges and Honduras Streets

BELGRANO

Just north of Palermo you'll find barrio Belgrano. This neighborhood has a dynamic mixture of old mansions, newer skyscrapers, beautiful high-rise apartment buildings and a university that keeps its leafy-green streets full of young faces. It's a popular shopping destination for porteños and is home to the Chinatown district on Arribenos street (in Bajo Belgrano), complete with Chinese restaurants, shops and a Buddhist temple. On January 22, the streets are doused in color and lights as the barrio celebrates Chinese New Year.

THINGS TO DO

Barrancas de Belgrano
This lush park, along with the majority of the rest of the neighborhood, was designed by Charles Thays, a French-Argentine architect. The Gazebo in the center is an especially good representation of Thay's artistic style. Jacaranda trees add swatches of purple to the park in the spring and you can enjoy live music, tango demonstrations, and artisan fairs which are held intermittently throughout the week.

Located in the center of Belgrano C

La Redonda

Inmaculanda Concepcion del Belgrano is a stunning church that is also known as La Redonda, meaning "the round one," due to its circular design. This church conducts many weddings throughout the year, and provides a great opportunity to see what a traditional Argentine wedding is like.

Between Calle La Pampa and 11 de Septiembre

ACCOMMODATION

Hostel Pampa

Pampa is conveniently located near the main drag in Belgrano (Avda. Cabildo) and offers bright, crisp, colorful paint throughout a colonial-style building, a great sun deck, private bathrooms in all of the dorms, a game room, study area, and complimentary breakfast and Wi-Fi.

Cost: 70–200 pesos

Ibera 2858 – Belgrano
+54 114-544-2273
info@hostelpampa.com.ar
www.hostelpampa.com.ar

SHOPPING

Avenida Cabildo

This avenue is one of the more popular shopping spots in Buenos Aires. Cafés, clothing shops, movie theaters and restaurants line the street. Expect to rub elbows with locals on the weekends because this area gets crazy busy Friday through Sunday.

SAN TELMO

San Telmo is one of the oldest and most charming neighborhoods in Buenos Aires. As such, it is also one of the most touristy. The cobblestone streets are lined with bars and boutiques, and the nightlife in San Telmo is chock-full of travelers. For this reason, it's a bit pricier than elsewhere in the city, but it's not quite as expensive as Palermo (yet).

THINGS TO DO

Plaza Dorrego
Lined with trees and cafés, this plaza comes alive on Sundays, when it hosts a large market from 10 a.m. to 5 p.m. During the day, and even more so after the vendors clear out, there is live music and dancing. The plaza itself is a sight any day of the week; it is the second oldest in Buenos Aires and hosts a number of beautiful sculptures and nearby historical landmarks.

Located on Humberto Primero and Defensa

Museo Historico Nacional

If you're a history buff, there's no better place to polish up and learn a bit more than here. The museum boasts a collection of artifacts from some of the city's most important historical figures, and the building itself has a beautiful interior, an observation tower, and two terrace gardens.

Defensa 1600
+(54) 0011-600-4307

ACCOMMODATION

Ostinatto Hostel

Boasting a modern design in a beautiful 1920s building, this hostel has got loads of appeal. The skylight gives the whole space a light, airy feel, and the modern design contrasted with the well-preserved original building is a work of art in and of itself. Five stories tall, this hostel offers loads of cool community spaces, including an artist's room on the fourth floor where Spanish classes are taught and artistic and musical exchange is encouraged. Ostinatto's prices are beyond competitive for the space and location, breakfast is included in the price, and the kitchen is especially clean and well stocked.

Cost: 70 pesos for a six-bedroom dorm room to 320 pesos for a private bath. They also offer a penthouse loft for 460 pesos a day, and if you book seven days in advance, you get a 10 percent discount.

From the bus station, Retiro, you *can take the C line or E line. From the C line, get off at the stop for Independencia. Walk three blocks east on Independencia and take a left on Chacabuco. Walk one block and turn right on Chile and you will find the hostel half a block down on your left. If you take line E, get off in Belgrano and walk three blocks south on Piedras until you intersect with Chile. Turn left and the hostel will be one and a half blocks. If it is late at night, we recommend taking a taxi for 20–30 pesos.*

Chile 680 – San Telmo
+54 114-362-9639
info@ostinatto.com.ar
www.ostinatto.com.ar

Pax Hostel

It's hard to go wrong with fresh-squeezed orange juice at breakfast, free international phone calls, and an awesome rooftop terrace. Plus, PAX is located on a well-lit street that is police-patrolled in the increasingly popular San Telmo district. They offer competitive prices, regular events, and a friendly and knowledgeable staff.

Cost: This is one of the best deals we found, with dorms for 50 pesos and private rooms for 90 pesos.

From Retiro, hop on the subte C line. Get off at Independencia and walk two blocks west to Salta. Take a left and walk two more blocks until you find the hostel on your left.

Salta 990
+54 114-305-1400
info@paxhostel.com
www.paxhostel.com

America del Sur

This modern hostel is clean, efficient, and popular. It offers almost more of a hotel feel, with loads of clean rooms. Each dorm has its own private bathroom, and the toilet, shower, and sink are all separate, which is awesome. There is a nice patio and a movie room downstairs, and tons of locker space both in the rooms and for rent in the basement, should you wish to store your things for longer. There is also individual heating and cooling in all of the rooms, which makes a huge difference in the summer and winter months. Rooms are slightly more expensive on the weekend, and prices vary slightly from season to season. We recommend checking online in advance. There is a 48-hour cancellation policy.

Cost: Dorms run between 60 and 85 pesos, and private doubles between 120 and 140 pesos.

From Retiro, take subte C line to Independencia. Walk east three blocks on Independencia until you reach Chacabuco. Take a left and you will see the hostel (tall grey building) on your right. If it is late and the subte is closed, we recommend taking a taxi for 20 to 30 pesos.

Chacabuco 718 – San Telmo
+54 114-300-5525
baires@americahostel.com.ar
www.americahostel.com.ar

······················· **SHOPPING** ·······················

Antique Market

Open daily, this market is in a huge hall hosting everything from fresh fruits and vegetables to vendors selling collections of antique matchbooks.

Near Plaza Dorrego on Defensa Street, between San Juan and Independencia

RECOLETA

Located between the center and Palermo, Recoleta is one of the city's older and most affluent neighborhoods. It has a number of interesting historical and tourist attractions, including a large 14-acre cemetery. For accommodation and shopping, Recoleta tends to be on the more expensive end of the spectrum, but as far as location goes, it grants easiest access to many of the other neighborhoods.

THINGS TO DO

La Recoleta Cemetery

The neighborhood's most popular attraction is a 14-acre cemetery filled with vaults—4,691 to be exact. Among them is the famous tomb of one of Argentina's most notable figures, Eva Perón. Entrance to the cemetery is free, and you can spend a better part of the day wandering the tombs. There are tons of options for food, drink and ice cream nearby, but they're definitely priced for tourists. If you're on a budget, we recommend packing your lunch and eating in one of the many beautiful parks located just outside the cemetery.

Open 365 days a year from 7 a.m. to 6 p.m.
Junín 1760
+54 114-803-1594
www.recoletacemetery.com.

ACCOMMODATION

El Sol Hostel

Located in the heart of Recoleta just off Avenida Santa Fe in a charming historic building, this hostel offers live music on the rooftop terrace most weekends, great pizza in the bar, and Wi-Fi in all the rooms. While it isn't equipped with all the bells and whistles as some hostels, what you pay for here is the location, and the friendly, knowledgeable staff.

Cost: Dorms begin at around 50 pesos for a six-person dorm and go up to about 120 pesos for a private room with a shared bath. In the summer, prices go up at least 10 pesos, sometimes more.

From Retiro, the easiest way to arrive is by subte, D line. Get off at Callao and walk two blocks north on Callao to Marcelo T. De Alvear. Turn right and walk two more blocks where you will find the hostel on the corner. In private taxi from Retiro, the trip will cost approximately 20 pesos.

Marcelo T. De Alvear 1590, 2nd floor
+54 114-811-6802
info@elsolrecoleta.com.ar
www.elsolrecoleta.com.ar

Recoleta Trip Hostel

This newer hostel offers a clean and vibrant atmosphere in a 1920s building, complete with a rooftop terrace and beautiful reading room with great views of the city. Breakfast, towels and airport pick-up are included in the price, and laundry and tours are available on-site. Wi-Fi is accessible in all rooms, and all rooms have shared bathrooms.

Cost: Five-bedroom dorms begin at 65 pesos, and prices go up from there to 200 pesos for a double room.

From Retiro, you can take the subte D line to Pueyrredon Avenue. Walk two blocks south on Avenida Santa Fe, and take a left on Azcuenaga. Walk seven blocks to Vicente López, take a right and the hostel will be immediately to your right.

Vicente López 2180
+54 114-807-8726
info@triprecoleta.com.ar
www.triprecoleta.com.ar

Petit Recoleta Hostel

The staff at Petit Recoleta are especially friendly and helpful. The hostel itself has a modern vibe in a beautiful 1920s home. The terrace and lounge spaces are comfortable and inviting, and Wi-Fi, breakfast, and towels are all included in the price. They also offer tango and Spanish lessons on site, and serve as a tour agency as well.

Cost: Basic six-person dorms begin at 65 pesos and private doubles run around 230 pesos.

From Retiro, jump on the subte line D and get off on Pueyrredon. Walk three blocks south on Avenida Santa Fe and take a left on Pte. J.E. Uriburu. The hostel will be on the right after the first block.

Pte. J.E. Uriburu 1183
+54 114-823-3848
info@petitrecoleta.com or
reservas@petitrecoleta.com
www.petitrecoleta.com

SHOPPING

Feria Atesanal de la Recoleta

For fantastic shopping, be sure to visit this fair, where you'll find everything from clothes and jewelry to souvenirs and mate gourds. This fair is pretty comparable to the one in San Telmo, but the vibe is really different, hosting more Argentines and a more affluent crowd.

Saturday and Sunday from 10 a.m. to 6 p.m.
Plaza Francia

EL CENTRO/RETIRO

If you're traveling in and out of Buenos Aires, you'll likely spend some time in Retiro, the city center, which houses the train and bus station. The area is a bit fast-paced and more seedy than other parts of Buenos Aires, but it's also home to some of the city's most well-known landmarks and some bargain shopping.

THINGS TO DO

Obilisk
Constructed in 1936, the El Obelisco de Buenos Aires is a national historic monument built to commemorate the fourth centenary of the first foundation of the city. A Buenos Aires icon and a great reference point for those who get lost easily, the monument is located in the Plaza de la República.

Intersection of Corrientes and 9 de Julio

Plaza de Mayo
Commemorating the May revolution that began Argentina's fight for independence from Spain, this plaza is often referred to as the political center of the city. The plaza can boast a history rich with protests and has been a stage for those voicing their grievances and sparking revolution. On one side of the plaza sits La Casa Rosada (the Presidential Palace), and on the other side is the Metropolitan Cathedral.

Located at the intersection of Hipóloto Yrigoyen, Balcarce, Rivadavia and Bolivar streets.

Teatro Colon
Known worldwide for its exceptional acoustics and the artistic value of its construction, Teatro Colón turned 100 years old in 2008. Recently renovated and in pristine condition, tours of the theater are worth the nearly 60 pesos. That being said, sometimes you can find tickets for shows at around 90 pesos, and it's worth the difference. Make a night of it and experience this incredible space through the performances it hosts.

Cerrito 628
info@teatrocolon.org.ar
www.teatrocolon.org.ar

ACCOMMODATION

Milhouse Youth Hostel

Occupying beautiful 19th-century homes, Milhouse hostels have earned their reputation as the party hostels of Buenos Aires. Both Milhouse hostels are located downtown in close proximity to major nightlife and many of BsAs main attractions. The rooms are clean and comfortable, and Wi-Fi and breakfast are included in the price. Laundry is also available on-site. In addition, Milhouse is one of the only—and maybe the only—hostels that organized events or activities every day of the week, and that sells tickets for major concerts, futbal games and exclusive clubs in-house.

Cost: Dorms begin around 65 pesos and go up from there to 340 pesos for a quadruple room.

Milhouse Hipo: *On subte Line C from Retiro, get off on Avenida de Mayo. Walk one block south to Yrigoyen, Hipolito and take a left. The hostel will be on your left. Alternatively, hop in a 10–15 peso taxi from Retiro.*

Milhouse Avenue: *Take the same subte line C from Retiro and get off on Avenida de Mayo. Continue walking west on Avenida de Mayo 2.5 blocks until you find the hostel on your right between Avenida Libertad and Santiago del Estero.*

Milhouse Hipo:
Hipólito Yrigoyen 959
+54 114-345-9604
www.milhousehostel.com

Milhouse Avenue:
Avenida de Mayo 1245
+54 114-383-9383
www.milhousehostel.com

Kaixo Hostel Central

Located just three blocks from the Obelisk in the heart of the city, this hostel offers a tranquil patio, awesome communal spaces, Spanish lessons, tango lessons, and tours from the hostel. The giant table in the dining room is conducive to meeting other travelers. Breakfast, Wi-Fi and towels are included in the price.

Cost: Dorms start at around 60 pesos and go up to about 220 pesos for a triple room.

From Retiro, hop on the C line to Diagonal Norte. Exit and walk three blocks west to Libertad and take a left. Walk one block and take your first right on Juan Domingo Perón. The hostel will be in the middle of the block on your right.

Juan Domingo Perón 1267
+54 114-383-9342
info@kaixobuenosaires.com
www.kaixobuenosaires.com

Hostel Estoril

In business for more than 10 years, the staff at Estoril know how to make your stay comfortable and easy. The hostel is located in a 100-plus year-old building with great views from the rooftop terrace and access to all the nearby attractions. Rooms are clean and comfortable, and the prices are competitive with other nearby hostels. The breakfast (included in the price) is more than just bread—it includes scrambled eggs, medialunas, juice and yogurt. There are two hostels located in the same building that are associated with Estoril, so don't get confused if you're directed up an additional five levels (or, request Terrazas Estoril if you are staying in a dorm and want the views!)

Cost: Six-person dorms begin at 60 pesos/person and prices go up from there to approximately 120 pesos for a private room located on the lower level of the hostel.

From Retiro, the easiest way to arrive is via subte on the C line. Get off at Avenida de Mayo and walk three and a half blocks to the west. The hostel will be on your right between Santiago del Estero and San Jose.

Avenida de Mayo 1385
+54 114-382-9073
info@hostelestoril.com
www.hostelestoril.com

SHOPPING

Florida Street

Pedestrian-friendly since 1913, with a longer stretch added in the 1970s, this store-lined street offers shopping for everything ranging from souvenirs, leather and clothes to food and electronics. That said, prices are generally a bit higher than they would be in Once or in markets in San Telmo or Palermo. If nothing else, when walking in the center, this is a great place to avoid traffic!

VOLUNTEER IN BA!

There are a ton of volunteer opportunities in Buenos Aires, including English teaching and working with the homeless. Find out more about volunteering on page 225.

CÓRDOBA

Córdoba is looked at as the little sister to Buenos Aires. It's one of the most distinct cities in Argentina, known for its adventure activities, shopping, and a friendly vibe. The people have an unusual accent with a sing-song cadence, and are friendly and warm. The amount of activities and beautiful satellite cities surrounding Córdoba, as well as a fully equipped metropolitan area, make it one of the most exciting cities in Argentina.

There's no shortage of things to do here—a number of festivals and special events take place throughout the year. If you can, dedicate *at least* a week to Córdoba. This will give you a chance to really take in what this vibrant city has to offer.

TOP ⭐ PICKS

Best Shopping:
The Handcraft Market on the weekends.
Awesome!

Best Hostel:
Hostel Morada

Best Out of Town Destination:
La Cumbrecita

THINGS TO KNOW

- From Humberto 1 to Avenida Costanera (where the river crosses the city) is, according to the locals, a dangerous part of town. Parque Sarmiento is also dangerous at night. If you can, avoid walking these areas at night. There is a lot of prostitution and crime.

- Carnival is in February, so make sure to do all of your booking in advance if you plan on visiting during this month.

- Córdoba is broken down into four main neighborhoods: Barrio General Paz, Barrio Alta Córdoba, Barrio Güemes and Barrio Nueva Córdoba.

SKYDIVING IN CÓRDOBA

Córdoba is known for its adventure activities, most notably skydiving. Find out more about skydiving by visiting www.skydivecordoba.com.

Think of an activity; the first thing that pops in your head. Yep, you can do that in Córdoba. The list of activities here is endless, so we won't bog you down with every little thing you can do, but to give you a taste: canoeing, skydiving, fishing, ecotourism, horseback riding, golfing, repelling, mountain biking, paragliding, scuba diving and on and on. You get the picture, right? The best way to go about partaking in these activities is to book one through your hostel. All of the hostels we recommended below are capable and willing to help you set something up.

Manzana Jesuitica

The Jesuit religious order settled in Córdoba in 1599, marking the city with a grouping of baroque-style buildings. Included in these is Iglesia de la Compania de Jesus, the oldest temple in Argentina, and Colegio Nacional Monserrat, the first university in Argentina.

Located on Avda. Obispo Trejo between Caseros and Duarte Quiros.

Parque Sarmiento

This park is located near the university and is a popular place for students to go between classes and sip on mate. The park has an amphitheater, a man-made lake with paddleboats, a zoological garden, skating rink and a fairground.

Parque Sarmiento is located southeast of Barrio Nuevo. Take General Paz from El Centro, heading south, until the avenue runs out.

Museo Ernesto Che Guevara

Visit the house where Ernesto "Che" Guevara spent much of his childhood, and find out more about his history. The house in Alta Gracia is 45 minutes outside of Córdoba. Take a bus to Alta Gracia and let your bus driver know to drop you off near the museo. Cost is 75 pesos for admission.

Avellaneda 501 - Barrio Carlos Pellegrini. Alta Gracia, Córdoba.
Tel.: +54 (0354) 742-8579
museocheguevara@altagracia.gov.ar

La Cumbrecita

This is one of the loveliest towns in the Córdoba province. The dirt roads, fragrant pine trees and meandering river provide a nice break from the arid desert climate that is prominent throughout most of northern Argentina. There are several hikes; you can either go on foot or rent a horse for the day and venture out into the immaculate hills and valleys surrounding the 800-person German town. Our favorite hike was to Cascada Escondida (Hidden Waterfall). It takes about four hours to complete, and takes you through constantly changing terrain.

Purchase a ticket at the bus terminal in Córdoba to Villa General Belgrano (about 55 pesos). The first bus (LEP is the company) leaves at 8 a.m., placing you in VGB at 10 a.m. From there, there will be (Pajaro Blanco) buses leaving every hour or so to La Cumbrecita (22 pesos).

Villa General Belgrano
Belgrano is located in the flourishing Calamuchita Valley. It was founded in 1930 by two Germans and has since been a main attraction to immigrants from Germany and Switzerland. People here speak German, there is German cuisine offered in the restaurants, German chocolate for sale throughout the village, and the architecture is straight out of, well, you know, Germany. It's a great place to visit for the novelty of it all, but you really only need a few hours to enjoy the town. As this is the connecting stop between Córdoba and La Cumbrecita, we recommend leaving Córdoba in the morning and purchasing your ticket for La Cumbrecita with a two or three hour delay, so you can wander around town a bit. The one time of the year you might consider staying the night in VGB is in October, when a proper Oktoberfest is held.

ACCOMMODATION

There are many hostels in Córdoba, but there are two main areas: Centro, which we preferred, or Nuevo Córdoba, the more modern section of town.

Centro

Baluch Backpackers Hostel
The thing that sets this hostel apart from others is the kind and extremely helpful staff. The majority of the employees, including the owner, speak excellent English and can set up almost any excursion you want to do in just moments. The space is smaller, but has all the amenities expected. The building overlooks busy San Martin St., where there are street vendors daily.

Cost: 60–70 pesos

San Martin 338, Córdoba
+54 (0351) 422-3977
service@baluchbackpackers.com
www.baluchbackpackers.com

Aldea
Aldea has one of the largest spaces in town; the exterior of the building does not do it justice. Inside you can find several large common areas with lounge chairs and a great outdoor patio with a colorful bar. It's older, but well kept.

Cost: 60–70 pesos

Santa Rosa 447
+54 (0351) 426-1312

hola@aldeahostel.com
www.aldeahostel.com

Link
Owned by two young, artistic professionals, Thiago and Santiago, Link is one of the newest hostel additions to Córdoba. The two have given an older building a complete face-lift and their space is beautiful, with tons of soft natural lighting and a mix of modern furniture and urban paintings and murals by Thiago. It is sparkling clean, and is one of the few hostels that has a dorm designated for women.

Cost: 60–70 pesos

Jujuy 267, Córdoba
+54 (0351) 421-6903
reservas@linkcórdoba hostel.com
www.linkcórdoba hostel.com

Morada Hostel
The brightly painted murals, multiple levels, and age of this large hostel give it a funky, warm feel. It is set a little away from the bustling streets and offers a great view from its spacious upper deck. Highly recommended, we had an awesome time here.

Cost: 55–70 pesos
Humberto Primero 532, Córdoba
+54 (0351) 421-6903
moradahostel@moradahostel.com
www.moradahostel.com

Nuevo Córdoba

Che Salguero Youth Hostel
There are currently two locations, but the newest one will most likely be around the longest. The hostels boast an urban-chic design and have great patios and common spaces.

Cost: 60+ pesos

Balarce 7576, Córdoba
+54 (0351) 421-3392
chesalguero@gmail.com
www.chesalguero.com

Le Grand Hostel
This chic hostel is one of the nicest in Argentina. It is spacious, convenient, and secure. There are gobs of dorm rooms available, and vacancy permitting, the staff will work with you to provide a female-only room. The stylish patio in the center of the hostel has everything needed to incite some serious socializing.

Cost: 60–350 pesos

Buenos Aires 547, Córdoba
+54 (0351) 422-7115
legrandhostel@gmail.com
www.legrandhostel.com

La Cumbrecita

Planeta Cumbrecita Hostel
This hostel is akin to sleeping in a cabin in the woods, in the best of ways. Its location and beautiful wood balcony allow for spectacular views of the town. The common area inside is finished in warm wood paneling and the rooms are small, but have large windows with views of the valley. Breakfast and Wi-Fi are included.

Cost: 75–180 pesos

+54 (035) 115-550-0847
planetacumbrecitahostel@gmail.
com
www.facebook.com/planetacum-
brecitahostel

SHOPPING

Patio Olmos
This large shopping mall has pretty much everything in it. But, you won't be able to bargain much.

Av. Vélez Sarsfield esquina Bv. San Juan

Handcraft Market

Every weekend, San Luis and Cañada Streets are home to an amazing handcraft market, full of locally made jewelry, clothes, shoes, art and much more. It's a must-see while in Córdoba. Don't miss it!

On San Luis and Cañada Streets

CENTRAL

If you're tired of Buenos Aires but don't have much time, head to the central provinces of Entre Ríos and Santa Fe. The provinces have both large cities, like Rosario, and small communities set on the river, like Paraná. Bring your mate cup and a thirst for relaxation—Entre Ríos has more than enough to keep you entertained, but there's also ample opportunity to enjoy doing nothing at all.

ROSARIO

Winding along the shores of the Paraná River, Rosario is the third largest city in Argentina, and boasts similar attractions as Buenos Aires, in a smaller and more accessible atmosphere. The river is the second largest in South America, and much of the city's industry and tourism take place on the shores of this magnificent river. Rosario has a reputation for being a cleaner, safer Buenos Aires, and boasts a beautiful populace. This is a great place to check out a growing modern art scene, and to visit the complex marine ecosystem created by the delta. It's also the birthplace of Che Guevara.

TOP ⭐ PICKS

Best Funky Hostel:
Art Rosario Hostel in Rosario

Best Place to Stop and Sip Mate:
Paraná

Best Place to Surf:
Mar de Plata

HOW TO GET THERE

Buses leave from Buenos Aires for Rosario frequently—almost every hour and cost between 130–170 pesos. The ride is about four hours.

Once you arrive in Rosario, hop in a taxi to your destination. You can try walking, but the city is pretty large.

THINGS TO KNOW

- Rosario's modern port is bustling and active as 78 percent of Argentina's grain exports take off from there. What does this mean for you traveling folks? Free Wi-Fi around the whole port area and in parts of the river as well.

- Depending on when you visit, keep your eyes out for the option of high-speed rail travel to Rosario. A high-speed train from Buenos Aires is scheduled for completion sometime in 2014.

- In the summer (September–December) Rosario is very hot and the sun is intense. Pack your sunscreen and plan on spending a good amount of time near or in the river!

National Flag Memorial or *Monumento Historico Nacional a la Bandera*

This 10,000 square meter complex pays tribute to the creator of the Argentina flag, Manual Belgrano, who first raised the flag in 1812. The site hosts three main parts: the 70-meter tall tower (the view from the top offers a great panoramic view of the city) which commemorates the Revolution of 1810, the Civic Courtyard and the Riumphal Propylaeum, which houses an Honor Room where all of the flags of are displayed. This is an impressive monument that is free to visit. It is especially beautiful at night, since a new lighting system was installed in 2007.

Museums

There are so many, we can't even begin to tell you about all of them. Museo de la Memoria, Museo Provincial de Ciencias Naturales, Museo de Arte Sacro, Museo de la Ciudad, Museo Municipal de Bellas Artes and many, many more. You could probably spend three days just visiting museums. Our advice is to stop by the tourist office, located on Avenida Belgrano y Avenida Buenos Aires, and get advice from them in line with your interests.

Parks and Beaches

There are plenty of beautiful parks to choose from in Rosario, but one of our favorites is Parque Independencia (between Pellegrini, 27 de Febrero, Moreno and Lagos streets). It's an old park that boasts 250 acres of mature trees, flowers, and special rose gardens, as well as two museums. The dancing water fountain is beautiful, especially in the early evening. Some other parks worth checking out are Parque Urquiza, Parque Italia and Bosque de los Constituyentes. Beaches are one of Rosario's most alluring attractions and La Florida is probably the most popular beach. There are lots of bars and kiosks around. You can also tote your own chairs and umbrellas to the beach, or opt to rent them for about 30 pesos for the day. If you dip into one of the bars on the beach, give *Clerica*, a popular local drink of chilled wine and fruit juice—a try!

Boat and Kayak trips on the River Paraná

There are a number of companies that run tours on the Paraná, and trips generally cost between 150 pesos for a guided kayak tour) to 250 pesos for a guided boat tour. Both are a great way not only to see the river but also to weave in and out of the many tributaries that make up this complex delta of the second longest river in South America. You'll see all kinds of wildlife, from birds to fish to capybara—an oversized swimming rodent that looks something like a giant guinea pig. Ask about beekeeping and stretch your legs with a trip to try some local honey on one of the islands.

ACCOMMODATION

Art Rosario Hostel

Aside from the awesome art that covers the walls of this hostel (you're invited to contribute), this hostel offers a fun and informed staff, great gathering areas, and a kiosk. It's located near the heart of the city, within walking distance of many of the main attractions. Breakfast and, get this—medical care—included.

Cost: The cost for dorms ranges from 70 pesos in the low season to 90 pesos in the high season.

The easiest way to get there is to jump a bus from the station and head toward the city center on Avenida Santa Fe. Jump off on Avenido Julio Presidente Roca and walk east two blocks. The hostel will be on your left.

President Roca 534
+54 (0341) 445-9759
elhostart@hotmail.com
www.artrosariohostel.com.ar

Rosario Inn Hostel

Just looking at this hostel is a treat in and of itself. It resides in a beautiful 19th century building with high ceilings, lots of exposed brick and great terrace spaces. The hostel is located in what is widely considered the birthplace of Rosario, with views of the river and the city. Many of the main attractions are just blocks away, and some less well-known but equally enticing attractions, such as the Centro de Expresiones Contemporánes, are just across the street. Breakfast is included and served all morning, and towels are also included in the price.

Cost: For shared dorms, prices are 50–60 pesos, and private double and single rooms range anywhere from 100 to 150 pesos.

From the bus terminal, you can catch any of the following bus lines and get off at Urquiza and Avenida San Martin: 101 negra y roja, 115, 121,116,146 negra y roja, 122 roja y verde, 120 y 128 roja. From there, head toward the water and take a left on Sgto Cabral. Stay to the left as you wind into the central plaza, and the hostel will be on the left, just before the intersection with Avenida Belgrano.

Sargento Cabral 54
+54 341-421-0358
info@rosarioinn.com.ar
www.rosarioinn.com.ar

Cool Raul

Cool Raul really lives up to its name. The place is really laid-back and relaxed, and just super-cool in general. Take part in one of the hostel's asados, or barbecues, and hang out on the roof and meet some mellow, like-minded people. You're practically guaranteed a good time.

Cost: 50–60 pesos

San Lorenzo 1670
+54 (0341) 426-2554
coolraulhostel@hotmail.com

www.coolraulhostel.com

La Comunidad Hostel

Bright, airy, and thoughtfully decorated, Comunidad offers large dorm rooms, clean bathrooms (some have tubs) and one of the best hostel bars we've seen. They also offer bike rentals and have a small patio gym. The building is nice and secure and the street it's located on has plenty of shops and restaurants.

Cost: 50–90 pesos

Presidente Roca 453, Rosario
+54 (0341) 424-5302
info@lacomunidadhostel.com.ar
www.lacomunidadhostel.com.ar

··· **SHOPPING** ·································

Alto-Rosario

Alto-Rosario is probably the most popular shopping spot in Rosario. This giant complex offers local, national, and international brands for all sorts of shopping, ranging from clothes and furniture to food and souvenirs. The train museum and children's museum are also located in this center, and the design of the center encourages a day of shopping ending with a casual afternoon coffee in one of the many neat cafés. While this spot has everything you might need, the prices are pretty standard with U.S. prices at an upper-end shopping mall.

Junín 501 – Rosario
+54 (0341) 410-6400

SANTE FE

Set right along the Rio Paraná, Santa Fe is the perfect place to come and relax for a few days. Stroll through the town to see 17th century Spanish colonial palaces and sip mate while taking in the natural beauty of the Sangre de Cristo Mountains. When you get tired of that, start walking around. Santa Fe is home to a plethora of shops and cafés—and even a casino—so you'll find plenty of ways to pass some time.

HOW TO GET THERE

The ride from Buenos Aires will take six hours and cost you roughly 65 pesos. From Colón, the ride is four hours and costs 52 pesos. The bus station is four blocks away from town center and it's easy to walk around Santa Fe. Pick up a map from the tourism office located in the bus terminal.

THINGS TO KNOW

- Santa Fe is definitely easy-going, and the city completely shuts down between 1 and 5 p.m. Come with an open mind and understand that things may not be done as quickly as you'd like them to be.

- There's only one hostel in town, but there are a few budget hotels around downtown.

- Santa Fe has a free bike rental system, and it's the easiest way to check out the town quickly. To rent a bike, head to the Ex Estación Ferrocarril Manuel Belgrano on Boulevard Galtrez and Avellaneda. You just have to sign in, show your passport and the address of where you're staying, and they'll provide you with a bike.

- For information on buses and colectivos while in the city, check out _www.colectivossantafe.com.ar_.

THINGS TO DO

Visit a Local Brewery
If you're into local beer, head to Cervecería Santa Fe and take one of their daily free tours of the brewery. Tours run at different times but almost always occur in the late afternoon or early evening. Stop by for more information.

Calchines 1401
450-2201
www.cervezasantafe.com.ar

Take a Boat Tour Down the Rio Paraná
Boat tours start in Dique 1 and go along a branch of the Rio Paraná. It's a relaxing way to spend an afternoon, complete with bar service and multimedia presentation. Tours are 40 pesos.

CostaLitoral Paseos y Eventos en Catamarán
Dique 1 – Puerto de Santa Fe
+54 (0342) 456-4381
www.costalitoral.com

Museo de Arte Contemporáneo
If you're into contemporary art, this small museum is located on the San Martin peatonal. The artwork changes every 15 days so there is always something new. Open Monday–Friday 8 a.m. to 12 p.m. and 4 to 8 p.m.

San Martin 2068
+54 (0342) 457-1885

People-watch on Boulevard Galvez
Don't forget to reserve some time to just take it all in—Boulevard Galvez is a great place to check out the area's cafés, shops, and scenery.

Read a Book
Advice Book Shop carries books in both English and Spanish, and has a large collection.

San Martin 3031
+54 (0342) 453-3392
www.advicebook.com.ar

ACCOMMODATION

Santa Fe Hostel

The only hostel in Santa Fe comes with free breakfast, Wi-Fi, and a clean kitchen area. It's small, and guests share one bathroom, but it's a good place to crash for a night or two.

Cost: 50 pesos for a shared room

From the bus terminal, turn right on Belgrano and walk 7 blocks. Turn right on Boulevard Galvez and the hostel is on your right.

Bv. Galvez 2175
+54 (0342) 455-4000
santadehostel@gmail.com
www.santafe-hostel.com

Nuevo Hotel Suipacha

Nuevo Hotel Suipacha has budget rooms and is located about halfway between downtown and Boulevard Galvez. Rooms are nothing special, but they're clean and will get you through the night. Unfortunately, they do not have a website.

Cost: 110 pesos

From the bus station, go straight on Hipólito Yrigoyen for one block, turn right on San Luis, walk two blocks to Suipacha and turn right.

Av. Suipacha 2375
+54 (0342) 452-1135

Hotel España

If you're in the mood to splash out and treat yourself to a nice room, this is the place for you. Owned by the same owners as the Conquistador Hotel across the street, this hotel offers better rates and still allows guests to use the amenities of the Conquistador: pool, gym sauna and solarium. Breakfast and Wi-Fi also included.

Cost: 235 pesos

From the bus station, go straight on Hipólito Yrigoyen for three blocks, turn left on 25 de Mayo, and the hotel will be on your right.

25 de Mayo 2647
+54 (0342) 400-8834
www.lineaverdehoteles.com.ar

SHOPPING

La Ribera

The main mall in town has a mix of clothing stores, an arcade, and a Cinemark theater playing current releases. Alternatively, walk along Boulevard Galvez and throughout downtown for smaller shops.
Dique 1 Puerto Santa Fe

PARANÁ

Paraná is the sleepy capital of Entre Ríos, set along the other side of the Paraná River from Santa Fe. Perched alongside the banks of the Paraná River, it's the perfect town to come get away from everything, and offers more riverside beaches than nearby Santa Fe. You probably won't stay long, since the town has little in the way of traveler's attractions—but that, in and of itself, makes it special.

HOW TO GET THERE

Buses run every hour between Paraná and Santa Fe and cost 4 pesos a ride. The bus terminal is a bit outside of the city center but it's a short walk to Plaza 25 de Mayo and the San Martín peatonal.

THINGS TO KNOW

- Like Santa Fe, the town shuts down between 1 and 5 p.m.

- The city center is easy to walk around, but if you want to get to the coast you'll want to take a bus or taxi.

- There is very little nightlife in Paraná. If you're looking to go out, take a taxi to the Puerto Nuevo area.

THINGS TO DO

Take a River Tour
For fishing trips and tours on the river, visit Costanera Viajes y Turismo. Tours begin at 30 pesos and become more expensive depending on what you'd like to do.

Buenos Aires 212
+54 (0343) 423-4385

Teatro 3 de Febrero
If you're in the mood for a show, visit this theater, a beautiful historical monument located only a few blocks off the San Martín peatonal. Their shows vary throughout the year but there are always at least one or two going on. The prices are low and

sometimes even free. Just walk by or call ahead to see what the current shows are.

25 de Junio 60
+54 (0343) 423-5701

Visit Museum of Mate
Nothing is more Argentine than mate, and the Museo Único del Mate pays tribute to one of the country's favorite drinks. Walk through seven rooms of different types and cups of mate through the ages. The unique museum is a fun way to spend some downtime.

25 de Junio 72
+54 (0343) 420-1814

········· ACCOMMODATION ·········

Paraná Hostel
One of only two hostels in Paraná, Paraná Hostel is located right in the city center. Free breakfast, bicycle rentals and Wi-Fi makes it a nice place to stay the night, and you'll likely meet other travelers in their communal living spaces.

Cost: 50 pesos

From the bus terminal, turn left on 25 de Mayo, right on Corrientes and left on Andres Pazos.

Andrés Pazos 159
+54 (0343) 422-8233
www.paranáhostel.com.ar

Paraná Art Hostel
Paraná Art Hostel is not as centrally located, but its amenities just about make up for that. Patio grill, free Wi-Fi and 24-hour drink service are all included.

Cost: 50 pesos for a shared room, 130 pesos for a private room.

From the bus terminal, turn left on 25 de Mayo, right on Belgrano/San Juan, left on Rosario del Tala.

Rosario del Tala
+54 (2430) 343-431-5597
Paranáarthostel@gmail.com
www.Paranáarthostel.com

SHOPPING

Feria del Pulgadas Peru 38

For cheap clothing and some handcraft goods, be sure to check out this small flea market on Peru 38.

COLÓN

A small town along the River Uruguay, Colón offers relaxing natural beauty and gorgeous beaches. If you have time, take a visit to the tranquil islands that surround Colón for a unique experience in this part of the country.

HOW TO GET THERE

Colón is located five hours away from Buenos Aires. From BA, the bus costs 100 pesos. It's four hours away from Santa Fe, which costs 52 pesos. The bus station is located close to the center of town.

THINGS TO KNOW

- Colón doesn't have much accommodation for a single traveler. There are no hostels here, and most places here have a bed for two, meaning it's a bit more expensive than other cities in the area.

- Eco-tours in Colón make it a gorgeous retreat for those who like the outdoors.

- Although it's a small, sleepy town, walking sometimes takes longer than it would elsewhere, as the blocks are pretty long.

- You can't hail taxis here, so you'll have to call one to take you around town.

- Colón is right on the border with Uruguay.

Lounge Along the Río Uruguay

The main thing to do in town is to chill out by the river. The beaches in town are super relaxing and make for a great place to sit and sip mate.

Visit the Geothermal Spas at Termas de Colón

If it's chilly outside, visit the geothermal spas, or *termas*, nearby. The termas has 10 indoor and outdoor pools ranging in temperature. It's a nice way to relax the day away. Open 9 a.m. to 8 p.m. 10 pesos.

Between 3 de Febrero and Lavalle
+54 (0344) 742-4717
www.termasdeentrerios.gov.ar

Parque Nacional Palmar

To get to this park, take a bus from the bus station for 100 pesos. The bus will drop you off 13 km. from the park, and you'll need to figure out how to get to it from there. Many hitchhike, but we don't recommend it. Alternatively, you could pay for a private car to take you there and drive you into the park for 200 pesos, or, if you have a group, book a tour through a travel agency for roughly 45 pesos per person.

Remis Palmar
Laprida 27 Colon Entre Ríos
+54 (0344) 742-1278
+54 (0800) 888-3280
Ask for "Parque Nacional Palmar Tour"

LHL Turismo
12 de abril 119 Colon, Entre Ríos
+54 (0344) 742-2222
www.lhlturismo.com.ar

Visit Remote Islands

Tours to Isla de Hornos, Banco de las Animales or Bancos del Carbillo offer different scenery, and tours cost roughly 110 pesos. There are several tour companies along 12 de Abril, so shop around to find what you're looking for.

ACCOMMODATION

Exit the bus terminal and take a right on Payansandú and you'll find most of the budget hotels.

Hostel La Casona de Susana

Located just two blocks from the beach, and close to most other attractions in the area, this hostel is your most affordable option. The place definitely leaves a lot to be desired, but there's a charm to it, and there are also female-only dorms.

Cost: 60 pesos

From the bus station just take a right on Paysandú and walk about 10 blocks, it will be on your right side.

3 de febrero 448
+54 (0344) 742-8043
info@casadesusana.com.ar

Hostería Restaurante del Puerto

This hotel doubles as a restaurant at night, and the food is tasty. You'll get your own room here, with air conditioning, maid service, TV, and a pool, but it's more expensive than a budget hostel.

Cost: A single room is 175 pesos, with doubles starting at 220 pesos.

From the bus terminal turn right on Paysandú then right on Peyret, the hotel is located between Chacabuco and Gouchón. It is several long blocks from the station, so if you have a lot of bags it is best to get a taxi from the terminal.

Alejo Peyret 158
+54 (0344) 742-2698
info@hosteriadelcolon.com.ar
www.hosteriadecolon.com.ar

Hotel Palmar

Hotel Palmar is located downtown, close to the beach and other attractions. All rooms include air conditioning, television, a breakfast buffet, and Wi-Fi. The hotel also has a pool and extra towels and robes if you want to go to the geothermal spas.

Cost: 180 pesos

It's a little too far to walk from the terminal, and your only other option is getting a cab from the terminal.

Boulevard Ferrari 295
+54 (0344) 742-1948
info@hotelpalmar.com.ar
www.hotelpalmar.com.ar

La Boutique de las Artesanias

This shop is a great place to look for souvenirs, including typical Argentine gifts such as leather key chains, mate gourds and jewelry. Prices are great.

12 de abril and Alem
+54 (0344) 742-3217

MAR DE PLATA

Mar de Plata is a national favorite for three-day weekends and holidays, which means the beaches get crowded very quickly. If you have some time and are hoping to escape from the hustle and bustle of Buenos Aires, it's a great place to get your feet wet and relax. The city boasts some beautiful beaches, fun art fairs, and interesting museums.

Buses leave from Buenos Aires for Mar de Plata frequently (almost every hour) and generally cost between 160–220 pesos for the 5-6 hour ride.

········ **THINGS TO KNOW** ········

* Local buses in Mar de Plata do not accept money, so stop into a local kiosko or the bus or train station to buy your tickets.

* As a regular hot-spot for Argentines, Mar de Plata is booked on holidays, especially in the summer. Always a good idea to book in advance, but especially during these times.

········ **THINGS TO DO** ········

Museo del Mar
All beached out, or get a day of bad weather? Check out the awesome collection of seashells from all around the world, and spend a minute pondering the tidal pool exhibit. Enjoy a coffee in the museum coffee shop, surrounded by floor-to-ceiling tanks!

Cost: 3 pesos.

Avenida Colon 1114.

Historic Homes on the Waterfront
Whether you're a fan of architecture or just enjoy looking at pretty things, a stroll along Barrio la Perla or Patricio Peralta Ramos Boulevard offers great views of beautiful Victorian summer homes.

Beaches
The beaches closest to town (Punta Iglesia and Playa Grande) are beautiful, but during summer months you may wind up fighting for a spot on the sand. Take a trek to Waikiki beach on the outskirts of town for a bit more room and more relaxation. Ever wanted to try surfing? Check out *www.kikiwaisurfclub.com.ar*.

ACCOMMODATION

El Refugio Hostel

This hostel has a really warm atmosphere and the common spaces were our favorite things. The front boasts a really neat front porch that is perfect for wine or mate hour, and the back yard is perfect for lounging, board games, etc. The rooms are pleasant and clean, and breakfast is also included in the rate.

Cost: The cost for dorms ranges from 50–80 pesos, depending on the number of beds in the room, and prices go up 10 pesos during high season.

From the new bus/train station: take bus line 541, which stops on Buenos Aires and Gascon. From there you can walk one and a half blocks east. The hostel will be on your left. From the old bus station, walk one block on Las Heras toward Gascon, turn left, and the hostel will be two blocks down.

Gascon 1831
+54 (0023) 495-6644
hostelelrefugio@gmail.com
www.hostelelrefugio.com

Casa Grande Hostel

Just four blocks from the beach and near the downtown, this tranquil hostel is located in the quiet neighborhood of La Perla. The staff and community spaces promote exchange between travelers. They have both mixed and female/male only rooms, and their double rooms with private bathrooms are a great deal.

Cost: For shared dorms, prices are anywhere from 50–60 pesos, and private double and single rooms range anywhere from 100–150 pesos. This hostel is a great deal.

Leaving from both the bus and train station, hop on a bus heading down Luro Avenue—the 511 or 512. As mentioned above, make sure to buy a ticket in the station, as buses do not accept cash. Head toward the ocean, get off at the intersection of Luro and Jujuy, and walk six blocks down Jujuy toward Libertad Avenue.

Jujuy 947
+54 (223) 476-0805
info@mardelplatahostel.com
www.mardelplatahostle.com

Hostel del Mar Backpackers House

Located in a beautiful old house just blocks away from the beach, this is a great place to hang out and chill, and also a great jumping-off spot for some of Mar de Plata's best activities, such as surfing. The kitchen is big and well equipped and the outdoor spaces are really nice. A giant picnic table in the back is always full of people sharing stories and making plans. Plus, they have bikes for rent and surfboard storage for anyone who brought their board along.

Cost: Prices range from 60 pesos for a dorm to 90 pesos for a double room for most of the year, except on holiday weekends when they jump to 75–130 pesos.

Just a short walk from the bus station, head down Calle Sarmiento until you reach Avenida Colon, and head just a few blocks toward the sea (east) until you find the hostel there on your left.

Avenida Colon 1051
+54 (0223) 486-3112
info@hosteldelmar.com.ar
www.hosteldelmar.com.ar

SHOPPING

Feria Central de Artesanos
In the civic center of Mar de Plata, check out the craftsmen's fair that got its start in the 1960s and now hosts more than 150 craftsmen. This is a great place to find some great handicrafts in a variety of materials from metal, wood, and cloth to ceramics and wax for reasonable prices.

The fair is open Saturday, Sunday and Holidays from 10 a.m. – 8 p.m.

Diagonal Pueyrredon between San Martin and Rividavia

Mercado de Pulgas – Antique Fair
Similar to its equivalents in Buenos Aires, this antique market has tons of diverse and beautiful antiques.

The fair is open Saturday and Sunday from 10 a.m. to 6 p.m.

Plaza Rocha between Avenida Luro and San Martin

NORTHEAST (LITORAL)

Northeastern Argentina, also known as the province of Litoral, is home to one of Argentina's biggest attractions: Iguazu Falls, a spectacular park with a waterfall that has recently been named one of the new 7 Wonders of Nature. No trip to Argentina would be complete without viewing the jaw-dropping scenery of Iguazu Falls, but there's plenty else in this area worth checking out as well. Looking for small towns, quiet rivers, stunning landscape and picturesque forests? You'll find it all here in Litoral.

TOP  PICKS

Best Stunning Scenery:
Iguazu Falls

Best Small Town:
San Cosme

Best Place to See Alligators:
Esteros del Iberá Wetlands in Mercedes

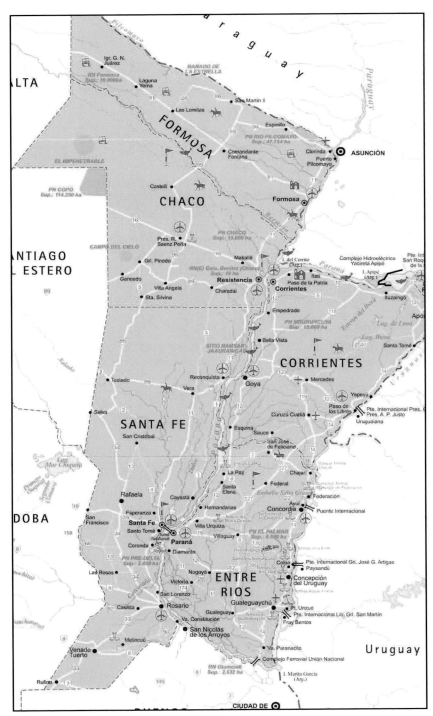

The main attraction in this area of Argentina is, of course, the unreal waterfalls, or Iguazu Falls, but the small town of Puerto Iguazu, located just minutes away from the falls, is a lovely place to spend your time until you hit the main park. The buildings are dripping in lush, overgrown tropical plants that offer the perfect backdrop to the many shops and restaurants that pepper the main avenues. We can see why this is such a tourist hot spot. As such, keep in mind that the prices here are pretty high.

HOW TO GET THERE

Buses leave frequently from Buenos Aires' Retiro bus station and take about 16 hours to arrive in Puerto Iguazu. If you can, try to avoid arriving at night. The bus costs about 575 pesos, but several bus companies run from BsAs to Iguazu, so shop around to find the best price. You'll be most comfortable with a cama or semi-cama seat.

THINGS TO KNOW

- A bus from within the town can take you directly to the gates of the park, where you'll be able to visit the falls.

- During hot summer months, remember to wear sunscreen and bring water. It gets really hot in the parks and you'll be doing a bit of walking to see everything.

- Special tours to the falls are unnecessary. Everything you want to see, you can see for yourself—at a fraction of the price.

- Iguazu Falls straddle the border between Brazil and Argentina. It is possible to see both sides in one day, but we personally feel the Argentine side has the most beautiful views.

THINGS TO DO

Iguazu Falls
The moment you approach the stunning and powerful falls of Iguazu, you will understand why this jungle oasis is such an attraction to travelers. The area is surrounded by jungle and toucans fly overhead as the fine mist of the falls creates a

dreamlike atmosphere. While you are unable to stray much from the structured trail system, the primitive surroundings offer a small window into what it must have been like to discover these falls for the first time.

The most economical way to travel to the falls is by bus. El Practico is a bus line that serves the Puerto Iguazu area. The buses are bright yellow and easy to spot. For only 10 pesos each way (a cab costs 170 pesos), you can catch a ride that takes about 30 minutes from the main bus terminal.

When you arrive at the park you will need to pay 130 pesos for general admission. Once you are inside, there are many tours you can pay for, but it is best to just navigate the park yourself. Grab a map and head out.

The must-sees are Paseo Garganta de Diablo and Paseo Inferior. If you have the time, we also recommend one of the boat tours (the cheapest costs 50 pesos). Give yourself at least four hours to tour the park, and be sure to check out times for boat rides, as they end pretty early. The train inside the park is free to ride and will save you some time.

You may be tempted to buy a rain pancho when you enter the park. It is unnecessary unless you are sure you are taking a boat ride that approaches the falls. Or, you know, if it's actually raining.

ACCOMMODATION

Hostel accommodations in this area are abundant and very similar to one another. However, we only found one that offered female-only dorms, so expect to pay a little more to get a private room if you don't care to bunk alongside guys.

Note: Private rooms can usually accommodate two people if you have a travel buddy to split the costs with.

All of the hostels we found in the one-mile radius surrounding the bus terminal offered a pool, Wi-Fi, complimentary breakfast, and air conditioning. Everything is just a short walk away, so if you haven't booked anything, walk around the town until you find a place you like.

Hostel Park Iguazu

About three blocks from the bus station on Paulino Amarante and Cordoba, this hostel is one of the least expensive and most charming of all. An outdoor, tropical common area is the first thing you see as you approach the entrance, and the rest of the hostel is equally as sweet. The rooms aren't anything fancy, but they are clean, and it is set far enough away from the main roads that it provides a tranquil atmosphere. They do not offer female-only dorms, but the price for a private room is very reasonable.

Cost: 50–170 pesos

Paulino Amarante 111-Pto. Iguazú (3370) Missiones
+54 (375) 742-4342
hostelparkiguazu@arnet.com.ar

Hostel Iguazú Falls

Just off of Missiones Ave., about two blocks from the bus terminal, sits the only hostel that we could find that offered female-only dorms. Make sure to book ahead as these rooms sell out frequently. The hostel boasts the same tropical atmosphere as its neighbors as well as an impressive patio area with a pool for its guests. Being able to rent a female-only dorm makes this one of the most economical and desirable hostels in town.

Cost: 60–180 pesos

Av. Guarani #70 Missiones
+54 (375) 742-1295
hosteliguazufalls.com

Hostel Bambu

Bambu offers two locations in town, Hostel Bambu Mini and Hostel Bambu Guazú, only moments away from one another. Our favorite was Mini: It's a little more off the beaten path and a bit hard to find, but it's also less expensive and quieter than Guazú. It offers everything the other location offers, other than a pool. If your budget allows, Gauzú is much newer and quite nice. Both only offer mixed dorms or private rooms.

Bambu Mini Cost: 150–250 pesos
Bambu Guazú Cost: 250–270 pesos

Mini:
Av. San Martin #4
+54 (375) 742-4864

Guazú:
Av. Cordoba 264
+54 (375) 742-5864
hostelbambu.ar@hotmail.com

SPLASH OUT AT IGUAZU GRAND RESORT

If you can afford it, consider staying at Iguazu Grand Resort Spa and Casino. The rooms are spectacular and nothing beats sitting by their gorgeous resort pool. There's also an indoor heated lap pool and spa.

Route 12 Km. 1640 (N3370AWT)
Puerto Iguazu. Misiones. Argentina
(54375) 749-8050
www.iguazugrand.com

SHOPPING

Because of how popular this destination is, shopping is expensive and touristy in Puerto Iguazu. That being said, if you see something you like in the bus station or in any of the small shops around the falls, buy it because you may not come across it again.

CORRIENTES

Corrientes is located on the eastern shore of the Paraná River. Although the city is substantial in size, it has a very laidback feel to it. The siestas are longer, scooters are packed on the roads in hoards, and you'd be hard-pressed to encounter someone *not* sipping mate on the street. Altogether, it's a great city to spend a day or two.

Along Junin (Peatonal Junin) you will find plenty of shopping opportunities and several plazas. The city also has some great cultural museums, and booms in the summer when it hosts Carnival, a festival much like the infamous ones held in Brazil.

THINGS TO KNOW

- Although this is a fishing town, it is hard to find fish in the restaurants. The best way to enjoy it is by purchasing it fresh on the river and taking it back to your hostel to grill.

- Corrientes enjoys an especially long siesta that runs from approximately 1 p.m. to 6 p.m.

- Motos (scooters) are a main source of transportation here but, unfortunately, you can't rent them for the day.

- Carnival is held in the summer from Feb. 11 through March 5.

- Both the sunrise and sunset over the river and General Belgrano bridge are stunning.

Visit the Esteros del Iberá Wetlands in Mercedes

The Esteros del Iberá wetlands are located in between Corrientes and nearby Mercedes. The Esteros are the second largest wetlands in the world, after those in Pantanal, Brazil, and amidst stagnant lakes, bogs, swamps and lagoons you'll find deer, two different types of Argentine alligators, and caiman.

Most choose to stay in Mercedes while visiting the wetlands. Several tours operate out of the small town. Visit the HI International in Mercedes or the tourist office within the bus station for information on tours.

THINGS TO DO

San Cosme

This small village is a short ride away from Corrientes. You can take a *combi* (a minibus or van) for 10 pesos from downtown. During the summer months Laguna Tortora turns into a lively beach where you can lounge by the water and have a drink, kite surf, or rent paddle boats. There is also a small center of the town where you will find some cultural markings and museums.

Head south on Mendoza from Junin, the main drag. It is necessary to ask for directions at this point, as there isn't always one exact place where they stop for pick up. Look for a collection of white vans. They will say "San Cosme" on the front.

Paso de la Patria
There are several beaches located along the river where you can get some sun, wade in the water, grill up some food and relax. Paso de la Patria is one of the more popular ones and is inexpensive to get to by combi.

Museo Historico de Corrientes
This museum has an impressive collection of art, antique furniture, and historical artifacts.

1044 9 de Julio.
www.welcomeargentina.com/corrientes/museo-historico

ACCOMMODATION

Hostel Bienvenida Golondrina
The only hostel in Corrientes is located less than a block away from the Paraná River. This beautiful early-1900s building has been carefully restored and turned into one of the most pleasant hostels in this part of Argentina. Golondrina offers pristine grounds, free Wi-Fi, complimentary breakfast, and lockers under the beds. The entrance is very secure and there is 24-hour staff. You can even borrow a bike to roam around town. It's best to take a taxi from the bus station as the walk would be quite long.

Cost: 70–200 pesos

La Rioja 455 – Corrientes Capital (3400)
+54 (378) 343-5316
www.hostelbienvenidagolondrina. com

SHOPPING

The bulk of the shopping can be found along Junin pedestrian street. Here you will mostly find clothing and shoe shops, music stores, and artisans selling their crafts on the sidewalk. There are also a few tents of shopping along the river where you can find inexpensive mate gourds and an array of other cheap finds.

FORMOSA

Formosa is probably not high on your list of places to visit, and we won't sugar-coat it—there's not a whole lot going on here. Set right on the Rio Paraguay, Formosa is the kind of place you end up while on your way to other places, namely, Paraguay. Nonetheless, if you find yourself here for the day, there are cafés throughout the town to keep you busy.

THINGS TO KNOW

• Formosa is located right next to the Paraguay border. As such, there is a heightened police presence in the area, searching for drugs that may have crossed the border.

• Foreigners staying in Formosa having crossed from the Paraguay border may be called into police quarters for questioning. There have been reports of long (5.5 hours) wait times for photographs and fingerprinting. This seems to be the exception and not the norm, but keep this in mind if you're just coming from Paraguay.

ACCOMMODATION

Asterion Hotel

This small hotel offers great service and clean rooms at a decent price. Hotel pool is nice as well. The only downside is that it's a bit outside of town. You'll need to catch a taxi to go back and forth.

Cost: 150 pesos or more

Acceso Sur, Ruta Nac. No 11 - Km. 1170
Formosa, Argentina
(0370) 445-2999/445-3933
info@asterionhotel.com.ar
www.asterionhotel.com.ar

Hotel Plaza

Set right on the Plaza San Martin in the center of town, Hotel Plaza is probably your best place to stay while in town on a budget. The rooms aren't anything to write home about, but there's a small swimming pool, which comes in handy when the humidity and heat get cranking.

Cost: 75 pesos or more

Uriburu 920
+54 (0371) 742-6767
hotelplaza@elpajaritosa.com.ar
www.hotelplazaformosa.com.ar

SHOPPING

While you can find some interesting Argentine and Paraguayan finds in Formosa, there's not a whole lot here to shop for. If you have time, cross the border and shop in Paraguay, as things are a bit cheaper there.

NORTH (SALTA)

The region of Salta is, to say the least, unlike any other. Here you'll find salt flats, tiny pueblos trapped in time, and Vicuna and Alpaca-smattered planes, all draped in a strikingly blue sky with the looming Andes Mountains as a backdrop. The city of Salta is an effective home base for sightseeing within the region, but as one of the largest cities in the north, offers plenty to see and do without ever leaving the city.

SALTA

Salta, the capital city of the region of the same name, is one of the largest cities in the north, though you'd hardly know it at first glance. With green parks, friendly people and beautiful plazas, Salta still feels like a small town, although its population is more than 500k. Here you'll find ample opportunities to shop, enjoy local street food, people watch and explore the greater region of Salta. Spend your days resting and preparing for more adventure—Salta is full of possibility and the options are endless.

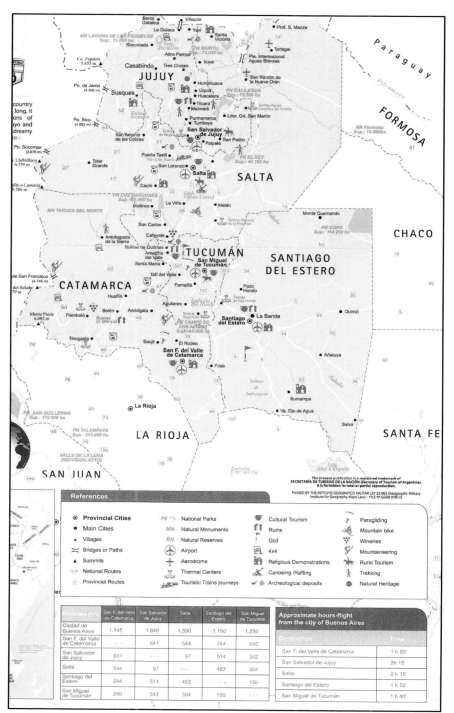

References

- ⊙ Provincial Cities
- ● Main Cities
- ● Villages
- ⋈ Bridges or Paths
- ▲ Summits
- National Routes
- Provincial Routes

- PN National Parks
- MN Natural Monuments
- RN Natural Reserves
- Airport
- Aerodrome
- Thermal Centers
- Touristic Trains journeys

- Cultural Tourism
- Ruins
- Golf
- 4x4
- Religious Demonstrations
- Canoeing /Rafting
- Archeological deposits

- Paragliding
- Mountain bike
- Wineries
- Mountaineering
- Rural Tourism
- Trekking
- Natural Heritage

Distances (km)	San F. del Valle de Catamarca	San Salvador de Jujuy	Salta	Santiago del Estero	San Miguel de Tucumán
Ciudad de Buenos Aires	1.145	1.640	1.590	1.150	1.250
San F. del Valle de Catamarca	- - -	641	544	244	240
San Salvador de Jujuy	641	- - -	97	514	342
Salta	544	97	- - -	482	304
Santiago del Estero	244	514	482	- - -	150
San Miguel de Tucumán	240	342	304	150	- - -

Approximate hours-flight from the city of Buenos Aires

Destination	Time
San F. del Valle de Catamarca	1 h 55'
San Salvador de Jujuy	2h 15'
Salta	2 h 15'
Santiago del Estero	1 h 55'
San Miguel de Tucumán	1 h 40'

TOP PICKS

Best Place for Natural Scenery:
Don't miss a visit to the salt flats, Salinas Grandes. Incredible!

Best Place to See Tango:
Cafayate

Best Hidden Small Pueblo:
Cachi

HOW TO GET THERE

As one of the largest cities in northern Argentina, it's easy to get to Salta from most areas. The bus station in Salta is new and beautiful, and it's not far from most areas of town. From Buenos Aires, the bus ride takes about 18–20 hours and costs between 300 and 450 pesos, depending on bus line. Salta is a large destination in the north, and you can get there from pretty much anywhere, so long as you're ready for some lengthy bus rides. The journey from Puerto Iguazu to Salta takes nearly 24 hours!

THINGS TO KNOW

- The people here are very generous and humble. Take the time to sit and have a conversation with a local.

- Salta is generally calm, with a large police presence in the streets. There is no need to get overly intimidated, but it's not a good idea to walk the streets alone at night.

- January and February are the rainiest months.

- *Humitas* and *tamales* are very similar, and you'll find them both here. They are both *masa* (corn dough) based and steamed in a cornhusk, but humitas only have masa, fresh corn kernels (and sometimes onion) and spices, whereas tamales might be filled with cheese, meat, chiles or other veggies.

• There are many churches and museums throughout Salta. Be sure to snag a map from the bus terminal or Teleferico to plan out your sightseeing.

THINGS TO DO

Salinas Grandes
One of the most popular excursions in Salta, this salt desert spans 3,200 square miles. The searing white landscape contains squares of exposed aqua-blue pools from the mining process (these flats are the source for the majority of salt consumed in Argentina). Once you arrive to the flats, there isn't much more to do than enjoy the view, which, like being in the snow, produces a piercing reflection that makes you susceptible to sunburn on your skin and eyes. Couple that with the altitude, and it can be a vicious source of ultra-violet damage, so be sure to wear sunscreen and sunglasses! For fun tours, check out www.argentina4u.com.

How to Get There: If you decide to do one of the day tours offered in town, you will most likely be picked up at your hostel, and will have little need to worry about directions. If you choose to go at it alone, there are a number of min-buses you can take, or you could rent a car and drive. Ask the front desk of your hostel for more info.

Catedral Basillica
This famous pink and yellow cathedral in Plaza 9 de Julio was destroyed in the 17th century and underwent a complete reconstruction, which was completed in 1882. It is the home to some very culturally important statues and tombs. At night it lights up and the entire building gives off a spectacular rosy glow.

Teleferico
This gondola, a short walk away from the bus terminal, deposits you at the top of San Bernardo Hill. It's easy to spend a couple of hours at the top taking in the views of the valley, meandering around the well-manicured gardens, complete with trickling waterfalls. There is also a small restaurant where you can have a beer or some tea and small market as well, and a workout area

where you can pump some iron and get your spin on. Costs 30 pesos, round trip.

Head left as you are leaving the bus terminal and you won't miss it.

Avda. San Martin and Hipolito Irigoyen

ACCOMMODATION

Hostel Salta Por Siempre
Por Siempre is a calm, spacious and friendly hostel. They offer a beautiful courtyard full of greenery and a two-tiered, artsy common room. The general aesthetic and vibe of the place is very laid-back. They have private dorms for women with a bathroom located in the dorm. It's a bit of a walk to downtown, but well worth it. All the usual amenities are included.

Cost: 60–200 pesos

Tucuman 464, Salta
+54 (0387) 423-3230
hostellingsalta@hotmail.com
www.saltaporsiempre.com.ar

7 Duendes Twin Hostel
The outside of this building is as immaculate as the interior. Only six months old, this hostel provides a multitude of new appliances and a long list of amenities. A great find in an older neighborhood. Wi-Fi, breakfast, full, modern kitchen, personal lockers, delightfully hot water and hairdryers included.

Cost: 35–50 pesos

Urquiza 1646, Salta
+54 (0387) 471-1158
www.7duendessalta.com

Backpacker's Hostel
Backpacker's Hostel is rich in character and amenities. The building is older and has definitely seen some better times, but is charming nonetheless. The hostel has several floors of common areas, including a great rooftop terrace, and one of the most attractive aspects; it has a restaurant/bar in the back that serves dinner (included in the rate) and hosts folk bands. There is also a great pool that is open during the summer months.

Cost: 60 pesos, dinner included.

Buenos Aires 930, Salta
+54 (0387) 423-5910
hostelsalta@backpackerssalta.com
www.backpackerssalta.com

Plaza 9 de Julio
This area of town is a bit more expensive than shopping in an outdoor market, but the stores are well organized and offer a better variety of shoes and clothing in colors and sizes that aren't as common in the other markets. There are also some great gaucho stores here that sell items that are finely crafted and nearly impossible to find at street markets, as well as some locally-owned jewelry and clothing shops where you'll find unique items to bring back home.

Marcado San Miguel
This indoor market has an amazing spread of clothing, spices, fresh produce, meats, cheeses, wine and more. There is also a food court where venders are cooking up some of the best and most inexpensive local dishes in town. We recommend the humitas and tamales – they were exceptional!

Avda. San Martin 750
Corner of Avda. San Martin and Ituzaingo
Hours: Monday to Saturday 7:30 a.m. to 2 p.m. (closed for siesta) 5 p.m. to 9:30 p.m.

Parque San Martin
Depending on the weather, you may find vendors selling out of booths just past the little lake in the center of the park, or you may find the brightly colored goods spilling right onto the walkway. Alpaca sweaters, Bolivian bags and tapestries, sunglasses, sandals and other trinkets can be found here on a daily basis, all available for a bargain. There is also plenty of great street food to enjoy (like dulce de leche filled churros).

Across from the bus terminal, Avda. San Martin and Santa Fe

CAFAYATE

Cafayate is one of the most romantic and relaxing cities in the north. It is well-known for its beautiful vineyards and rural surroundings, and the town is so calm and tight-knit that it is not uncommon to see unlocked bikes scattered up and down the dirt roads. If you're into vineyard tours, there are plenty to be had—or you can just wander the tree-lined town by foot or on bike and enjoy some truly great meals. The summer is the best time for vineyard hopping, but the fall offers crisp breezes, rustling, colorful foliage, and fewer tourists.

THINGS TO KNOW

- Many of the restaurants in the square offer excellent fine dining experiences. Expect to pay around 100–150 pesos altogether, but this price includes exceptional food and a few glasses of amazing local wine.

- Buying wine from a market will always be cheaper than buying it at a restaurant. If you want to save some money, have *one* glass with dinner to complement your food, then pick up a bottle afterwards and take it for some balcony time at your hostel. While Argentina is usually associated with its red (*tinto*) malbec wine varieties, the torrontes white (*blanco*) wine in Cafayate is one of the main wines of the region and it is fruity, smooth and delicious. Our favorite label was Quara.

- There are endless places to rent bikes in this town (including most hostels and hotels) and we highly recommend that you do. It is one of the best ways to really take in all the beautiful sights and smells of this earthy town.

- Helideria Miranda, located on Av. General Guemes, is known for their wine-tinted ice cream in flavors like cabernet and torrents.

THINGS TO DO

Bodega Nanni
Bodega Nanni has been run by the Nanni family since 1897. One of the Nanni family's philosophies is having respect for the earth that they grow their grapes on, so all the growing is done organically at their vineyard. The tour of the bodega is informative but not overbearing, and the cost is minimal at 5 pesos.

Museo de la Vid y el Vino
This very modern museum, located on Av. General Guemes and Chacabuco, is a stark contrast to the rest of the earthy, matured pueblo. The museum houses a wine boutique and a small historical room with artifacts from old bodegas. The entrance fee is 30 pesos.

La Garganta del Diablo/El Anfiteatro
Garganta del Diablo is an ancient red rock formation in Valle Calchaqui along Rio las Conchas. Just a mile or so up the way from Diablo is El Anfiteatro, a natural amphitheater. In the summer, concerts are held here, showcasing the natural acoustics created by the surrounding red rock walls. The best way to explore this area is to take a minibus to the top, then rent a bike and jam down the hill through the red rock ravines back to Cafayate. It's a 25-mile ride, but it's downhill—so no problem, right? Make sure to keep to the main road if you want to avoid a flat tire, and be wary of cars and motorbikes zipping by.

ACCOMMODATION

El Balcon International Hostel
This beautifully designed hostel has one of the best terraces in town. From the ground, this two-level balcony looks like it belongs to a nice restaurant. The rooms here are well maintained and there is a great room upstairs that has a large kitchen and common area

complete with cable TV and computer station. The staff is also extremely nice and quick to help you navigate the town or arrange an excursion.

Cost: 30–70 pesos

Pasaje 20 de Febrero 110, Cafayate
+54 (0386) 842-1739
info@elbalconhostel.com.ar
www.elbalconhostel.com.ar

Hostel Ruta 40
Located just a block away from the main square, Ruta 40 is a smaller hostel, but the staff is extremely warm and inviting. The rooms have a lot of character and there is a nice café-style patio, perfect for sipping coffee and chatting with the staff and other travelers. They also have a small bar that offers happy hour, a grill, and fully stocked kitchen and bicycle rentals.

Cost: 55–240 pesos

Av. General Guemes 178, Cafayate
+54 (0386) 842-1689
www.hostel-ruta40.com

SHOPPING

Most of the shopping in Cafayate can be found around the central plaza. There is also a great set of shops as you follow Av. General Guemes towards the Museo de la Vid y Vino.

CACHI

Cachi was built before the Spanish domination and was once home to the local *Chicoanas*. The small white town is like something off of a postcard: cobblestone streets, adobe houses and small indigenous churches, backed by a gorgeous mountain range set within the Chalchaquí Valleys.

Its remote location makes it all the more appealing to travelers. To get here from Salta, you'll have to brave the winding four-hour road, some of which is unpaved. The rewards are well worth the effort, though. Cachi is the kind of place that puts you at ease, and keeps you much longer than you planned.

HOW TO GET THERE

To get to Cachi, you have essentially two options: Take a tour or drive.

From Salta, you'll take Route 68, and then Route 33. Keep in mind that much of this road is unpaved.

From Cafayate, take Route 40. This is a gorgeous road trip if you have a car. You'll pass through the Gorge of Arrows and then into the small villages of San Carlos, Animaná, Yacochuya, Molinos and Seclantás.

THINGS TO KNOW

- Cachi is a very small village. It's possible to see the entire town in one day just by walking, but if you have time, spend the night—you'll see what the town is really like after most travelers have left.

- Although it can be very hot during the day, Cachi can get cold at night. Bring a sweater!

- Cachi means salt in Quechua. The natives mistook the top of "El Nevado," near the village, for a salt mine.

- Visit the tourist office in the main plaza for information on what to see in the area and where to stay.

Parque Nacional Los Cardones
This national park offers you a great look at the desert scenery. Although, you'll be able to take in much of what the park has to offer just by walking around the area.

Iglesia de San Jose
The main church in Cachi is beautiful and is well worth a visit.

Walk Around the Town
Half of the fun of Cachi is just exploring what's in the small village. Take a stroll, and don't forget to bring your camera.

········· **ACCOMMODATION** ·········

Cachi is very small, so most places don't have a phone number or website. Just ask at the tourist office for information.

Camping Municipal
There's a local camping area with no name or address in town. Just ask locals where you can camp and they'll point you in the right direction, about 1 km. south of the main plaza.

Cost: 20 pesos

Alberque Municipal
Rent a bed in a hostel through the tourist office in the main plaza, Plaza 9 de Julio.

Cost: 20 pesos

Hosteria Cachi
Comfortable rooms, beautiful views, and a pool! Hosteria Cachi is a bit more expensive than the no-thrills 20 pesos dorm bed, but is well worth it. A great place to splash out for the night.

Cost: 50–75 pesos

Route 40/ kilometer 1,237
+54 (03868)/491-105
+54 (03868) 491-904
www.soldelvalle.com.ar

IRUYA

This small town in the Salta Province was built directly into the mountainside at an altitude of more than 9,000 feet. In the wee morning hours, you can spot gauchos preparing their horses and mules, workers walking down the steep, narrow cobblestone paths with pick axes and shovels thrown over their shoulders, and dogs scattering across every nook and cranny looking for a pack to join, human or canine.

The nights are set among the most majestic surroundings as the Andes Mountains, crowned with low-hanging clouds, tower around the small pueblo. The moonlight creates an eerie glow as it bounces off the low-lit adobe houses and stone walls, and simply put, this place is amazing. It's a rare look into an almost untouched society in one of the most unusual places in the world.

HOW TO GET THERE

The only access to Iruya is by bus from Humahuaca (even if you've rented a car, we wouldn't recommend trying to drive the small, windy roads that lead to Iruya). The bus ride isn't long, although it may feel endless when you are turning corners on one-lane dirt roads with steep drop offs. Bus ride is 54 pesos.

THINGS TO KNOW

- Surprisingly, there *is* an ATM in town.

- Keep your eyes to the sky and you might catch a glimpse of an Andean Condor or two.

- Make sure to ask the locals nicely if you can take their picture. You will probably upset them if you just run around snapping shots without permission. Also, be ready to pay a few pesos in return.

THINGS TO DO

San Isidro
About a five-mile walk from the main pueblo along a trail that winds through the towering Andes mountains and across riverbeds and through a small indigenous community is San Isidro, a pueblo of approximately 350 people. There is a great teahouse to stop for lunch and a market that sells some great regional crafts. The pueblo is enchanting but the walk is well worth it for the views of the Andes alone.

How to Get There: From Iruya's town square, head towards the river and use the path to cross it, you will see a sign that guides you, but there is really no way to get lost as the trail is clearly marked.

ACCOMMODATION

Casa de Familia Asunta
This family-run place is not listed in many hostel resources, but it is one of the coolest hostels in the north. The hostel is multi-tiered and offers a few dorm rooms and a couple private rooms as well. The bathrooms are toilet/shower combos, but they are newer and clean, and the rooms are simple with soft beds. Everything is well kept and the views from the terrace are spectacular. No Wi-Fi (yet).

Cost: 30–70 pesos

As you walk into town from the bus stop, going uphill with the stone wall on your left side, you will make your first left onto Belgrano and follow the hill up until it nearly ends. On the left you will see a small sign for Asunta connected to their large terrace.

Belgrano
+54 (0387) 15 404-5113
hospedajeasunta@gmail.com

Unfortunately, none of the hostels here include breakfast or Wi-Fi.

Milmahuasi Hostel
A little lower on the mountain, but with great views of the river, you will find Milmahuasi hostel. It is a little pricey for the area, but has large rooms, three of which offer private bathrooms.

Cost: 60–120 pesos

Calle Salta (just before Retiro)
+54 (0387) 15 445-2883
milmahuasi@hotmail.com
www.milmahuasi.com

SHOPPING

San Isidro
There are several artisan shops scattered through Iruya, but we recommend San Isidro for any crafts purchases.

CATAMARCA

Catamarca is a city located in the province of the same name. Despite its quick growth, Catamarca isn't yet very accommodating to travelers. That isn't to say that the people here are unfriendly or that there is nothing to do or see, but there is a limited amount of accommodation, and most of the sites are located outside of the city. The town is laid out in in the grid system that is common throughout Argentina, with the main square in the center, complete with a park, cathedral and several museums.

THINGS TO KNOW

- The hostels here are a bit peculiar and the maps that are available at the bus terminal aren't very accurate. We followed the maps to many hostels that seemed to not exist, and the ones that did were more like family homes or local hangouts that seemed a little unwelcoming.

- In late July, the town hosts *La Fiesta Nacional del Pancho*, a festival that highlights the tradition of vicuna and alpaca panchos from the region. Colorful attire, folk bands and food can be found in the main plaza.

- The bus terminal here has a movie theater, so if you are delayed you can pass the time in a dark theater.

THINGS TO DO

La Virgen del Valle Cathedral
A very impressive neoclassical cathedral is located in the main plaza. The cathedral has undergone restorations, but has been preserved in the original style that it was created in.

Museo Arqueologico Adan Quiroga
This museum is definitely one of Catamarca's more impressive assets. Glass cases are filled with indigenous tools, jewelry and other artifacts and there is a large collection of pre-Columbian pottery on display.

From the main plaza, head north on Sarmiento and follow it past Esquiu and you will see the museum on the right-hand side of the street. Sarmiento 450

ACCOMMODATION

We visited all of the hostels available at the time, but most seemed unorganized and unsecure. If you want to stay here overnight, we recommend splurging on a hotel.

Amerian Catamarca Park Hotel
The Amerian is located just up the street from the main plaza. It is modern, clean and has all of the amenities you would expect out of a four-star hotel. There is also a gym, sauna and pool (often closed during the fall and winter months) and breakfast, cable, A/C and Wi-Fi are included. The building is really secure, and there is 24-hour staff.

Cost: 400–600 pesos

Republica 347, Catamarca
+54 (0383) 342-5444
reservascat@hotmail.com
www.amerian.com

SHOPPING

Virgen del Valle
There is an artisanal market on Virgen del Valle where you can find an array of regional crafts and goodies. Panchos are abundant here due to the fiesta held in July, and can be found in a variety of colors and styles. You can also find local nuts, olive oil and wine.

Av. Virgen del Valle 945

NORTH (JUJUY)

You may have heard from other travelers by now: the region of Jujuy is simply stunning. Be aware, however, it's the region, not the city of San Salvador de Jujuy, that they're referring to. The city of Jujuy is a small and urban, without a whole lot to offer to travelers, but the region is *muy magnifico!* Here you'll find vast fields of sunflowers, the incredible *Cerro de Los Siete Colores* (the hill of seven colors), and small pueblos full of friendly faces. Give yourself at least a few days to explore this gorgeous region—you won't regret it!

TOP  PICKS

Best Place for a Sunset:
Purmamarca. Watch as the Cerro de Los Siete Colores changes in the light.

Best Small Village:
Tilcara

Best Place to Talk Politics:
San Salvador de Jujuy

NORTE MAP

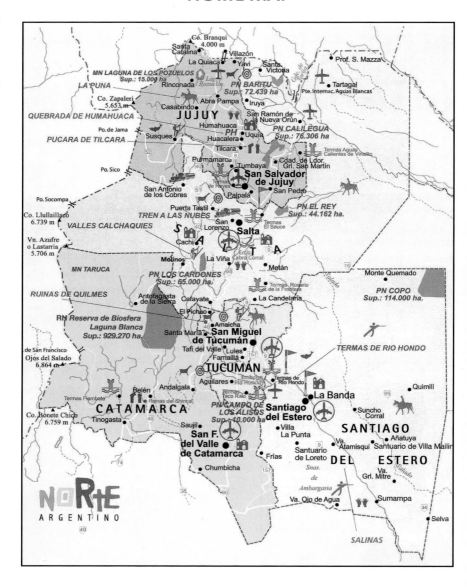

SAN SALVADOR DE JUJUY

Of all the cities in Jujuy province, San Salvador de Jujuy (commonly referred to simply as Jujuy) had a smaller number of impressive buildings and museums, but it seemed to have the greatest amount of political charge, which made it stand out as an excellent place to sit in on a coffee-shop discussion amongst locals about the current state of affairs in Argentina. We thought maybe it was just our specific experience here, but after talking to locals and witnessing a few peaceful demonstrations in the street, we concluded that the level of political savvy that the people in Jujuy have is indeed unique. And of course, we should mention that the rural areas outside of the main city were beautiful as well, with some great hiking opportunities should you decide to make Jujuy more than just a day trip.

THINGS TO KNOW

• Black and red graffiti with simple but deliberate political messages adorn the walls of many buildings. Take the time to translate the messages; some of them are pretty cool and informative about some of the current political issues in the area.

• The city is influenced by the cultures of the Quechua, Aymara and Chiriguano, and it is common to see things written in Quechua around town.

• There are currently only two hostels in the city of Jujuy.

THINGS TO DO

Cementerio El Salvador
Even though it's only a fraction of the size, this beautiful cemetery manages to rival the world-famous Recoleta cemetery in Buenos Aires. Elaborate tombs and headstones are covered in decades of moss and the sound of pigeons flying through halls of stacked graves only add to the unusual mix of eeriness and calm that hangs in the air at El Salvador.

Plaza de Belgrano
Like many of the other cities in the north, Jujuy is on a grid and has a main square located in the center of town. Here you will find street vendors, shops and restaurants and the Iglesia Catedral Basilica.

ACCOMMODATION

Yok Wahi Hostel & Bar
The owner of this hostel recently moved from another location just down the street by the same name. When he decided to move his successful business to a more modern building, it led many a backpacker astray due to the old address in older guidebooks. After seeing the new location, which had an Irish pub feel to it, complete with beautiful green and blue stained glass windows and a wood bar that carried an array of imported beers, it was clear why he chose the new digs. The rooms here are spacious with high ceilings and there is an outdoor patio that is under-going some exciting updates. Once this hostel is complete it is sure to be extremely popular, so make sure to reserve a room in advance!

Cost: 40–80 pesos

Independencia 946, San Salvador de Jujuy
+54 (0388) 422-9608
reservas@yokwahi.com
www.yokwahi.com

Club Hostel
The vibe at Club Hostel fits the name. Throughout most of the day, club beats are being pumped through speakers all over the hostel. It had the general feeling of a college dorm and seemed to be popular amongst the 18-25 crowd. They offer a large number of dorm rooms (female-only on request if vacancy permits it), a Jacuzzi and outdoor bar, and an attached office that offers booking assistance for excursions and bus tickets.

Cost: 65–80 pesos

San Martin 134, San Salvador de Jujuy

+54 (0388) 423-7565
clubhostel@noroestevirtual.com.ar
www.noroestevirtual.com.ar/club/
hostel.htm

SHOPPING

Paseo de Artesanias

A typical northern crafts fair takes place seven days a week along Sarmiento.

Cerro de los Siete Colores, Purmamarca -- photo courtesy of Chris Kilgore

PURMAMARCA

You've probably seen those postcards of the multicolored mountains of Argentina, which sit at the foot of the small northern town of Purmamarca. The *Cerro de Los Siete Colores* (Hill of Seven Colors) attracts visitors year-round, who come to photograph as the mountain changes from dawn to dusk. The views are spectacular, much of the accommodation is resort-like, and the crafts fair is chalk-full of Bolivian and Argentine goodies.

THINGS TO KNOW

- This small pueblo is a great place to enjoy some of the regional cuisine, such as goat's cheese and llama meat.

- There didn't seem to be any specific hikes to take, but the hills are a hop, skip, and jump away from the town and any walk you take is sure to be beautiful. We recommend sunset, as this is when the colors on the hills are most vivid.

THINGS TO DO

La Iglesia de Santa Rosa
This rustic adobe church houses paintings that date back to the 18th century. A festival is also held in town on Aug. 30 to celebrate Saint Rosa.

ACCOMMODATION

There weren't a lot of inexpensive hostels during our visit to choose from, so if you want to stay the night here, consider treating yourself to one of the hotels or head to nearby Tilcara.

Hostal Posta de Purmamarca
This rose-colored adobe and stone building is located a little up and away from the town square, providing a quiet resort-like atmosphere. The grounds are immaculate and showcase a variety of local cactus and succulents. The back of the hostel faces the mountain, and provides a great location to have breakfast or coffee and enjoy the breathtaking views. But pampering like this doesn't come cheap! A really nice

continental breakfast is included in the price of the room, as well as LCD TVs and Wi-Fi.

Cost: 240–400 pesos

La Banda, Humahuaca (Just across the bridge to the right)
+54 (0387) 715-587-8136

SHOPPING

Crafts Fair

This large crafts fair in the town square is absolutely brimming with colorful tapestries, ponchos, shoes and more. The stores surrounding it are also amazing, and competition is high so there is minimal fluctuation in the prices and a little budge room for bartering; especially if you plan on buying more than one of any item.

TILCARA

Located in the Jujuy province surrounded by the Andes mountains is Tilcara, a quaint and tranquil town. The streets are unpaved and the buildings are beautiful but humble, much like the locals. Gusts of wind are trapped in the valley and small clouds of dirt rise and fall onto the stone streets. At night, the clear skies and high elevation (2,500 meters above sea level) offer spectacular views of the stars. Tilcara is rich with indigenous Inca history, colorful handmade crafts, and amazing food. The location and spirit of this town provide a wonderful feeling of seclusion from the rest of the country. It is small, but not to be missed.

THINGS TO KNOW

- There is an abundance of live music here both day and night. Traditional bands that use wind instruments, as well as more modern folk bands, are both common.

- Many of the traditional dishes here are vegetarian, which is rare for Argentina. If you don't eat meat, or you are just in need of a change, this is the perfect opportunity. Favorite dish: *Carbonada en Calabeza*—veggies roasted in a pumpkin then topped with local cheese and scallions.

- There is a folklore music festival here in the second week of January and Carnival is celebrated in late February. As the town is so small, hostels are booked solid during these events. Be sure to book in advance if you are staying during these popular months.

- Buses run from any of the major surrounding cities into Tilcara. The bus ride is inexpensive and once you arrive at the town, you will see how simple it is to navigate. Make sure to pass up the hostels that are located right outside of the terminal; they are inexpensive, but for an extra 10-20 pesos more you can have better accommodation on Calle Padilla.

Garganta de Diablo

"The Devil's Throat" is a massive canyon at the upper part of the Huasamayo River. In addition to its energizing landscape, this canyon also holds petrified trilobites (fossils) that can be found in the incisions in the rocks. Once you get to the top, there will be a small building where you can pay a few pesos to venture down into a portion of the canyon where a small natural waterfall can be found.

From the bus terminal, head to Belgrano Street and follow it to Padilla. Make a right on Padilla and follow it as it curves to the right. You will see the Puente bridge almost immediately. Instead of crossing the bridge, follow the path to the right. There are signs along the way to keep you on track.

Pucará de Tilcara/Botanical Garden

Just a short walk away from the main town, you will find this impressive reconstruction of pre-Inca ruins. The artifacts from this location are held in a museum in Humahuaca, but the fabricated rooms give insight into the way the town originally looked and the location offers vast, impressive views of the valley and surrounding mountains. As you enter the site you will also have a chance to view the botanical gardens that display various species of native cactus.

Follow the same directions as those to Garganta de Diablo, but cross the bridge and follow it until you see a small strip of shops. Here you will find the entrance to the botanical gardens that leads to Pucará de Tilcara.

All of the hostels we liked were located on Calle Padilla, just a short walk from the bus terminal; from the terminal, take Belgrano St. to Padilla, and head right. The look and feel of each hostel is unique, but the amenities were pretty identical. Breakfast, lockers, kitchens and Wi-Fi were offered at all three locations. All of the dorms are mixed, but the staff will usually work with you if you prefer female-only.

La Albahaca Hostel

This multi-leveled hostel had the feel of an Italian café, and included a beautiful rooftop terrace. The rooms were a little larger than the other hostels and they had a suite that could be shared between several people that had a private bathroom and adorable balcony. The owner was very hospitable and it felt very female-friendly. As most of the hostels in town are about the same price, this is our top pick.

Cost: 30–100 pesos

Calle Padilla 731, Tilcara
+54 (038) 815 585-5994
info@albahacahostel.com.ar
www.albahacahostel.com.ar

Hostel Waira

Set on a rather large area of land, this hostel is likened to camping in cabins. The rooms are really old but well-kept, and the shower definitely leaves something to be desired, but the grounds are earthy, honest and reflect the rest of the town. Waira also reserves a portion of its grounds for campers (bring your own tent) at a low cost. If you are not too finicky about amenities, this hostel makes for a great, down-to-earth experience.

Cost: 30–100 pesos

Alverro 276, Tilcara
+54 (0388) 495-5154
hostelwaira@gmail.com
www.hostelwaira.com.ar

Tilcara Mistica Hostel

The murals, music and grass-roof bar in the front courtyard of Mistica give the hostel a rasta esthetic. While we were here, they were undergoing some construction for what looked like a promising new lounge area. The bathrooms have a shower/toilet combo, which is never ideal, but they were clean and the water was hot. The rooms are small but tidy, and the staff is super-friendly.

Cost: 30–100 pesos

Padilla 575, Tilcara
+54 (9223) 689-0346
tilcaramistica@gmail.com
www.facebook.com/tilcaramisti-cahostel

If you have been eyeing the stacks of alpaca goods that can be found in most of northern Argentina, you've arrived at the very best spot to purchase them.

El Plaza Central

Located on Belgrano, you can find a mixture of Bolivian and Argentine craft items at really low costs. In the main square there is a daily market where you can stroll by the tents and find handcrafted bags, sweaters, mittens, jewelry and more.

Bartering is common, but try not to ask for more than a 10 to 20 percent discount as the prices here are already so low (you don't want to insult the vendors).

Feria de Artisanias

This fair takes place on Saturdays, located in a building on Rio Huasamayo. It is similar to a swap meet and has mostly second-hand items. The most impressive section has fresh local produce, herbs, and meat (including llama).

HUMAHUACA

Humahuaca is similar to the neighboring pueblos of Purmamarca and Tilcara, but it's livelier, if not a bit more gritty. The narrow cobblestone streets are lined with graffiti-adorned adobe buildings that display decaying painted doors, but there's a charm here that you can only find traveling through northern Argentina. The town itself is small and can be walked in a couple of hours, but it's home to a sizeable population, so there's a distinct hustle and bustle that will keep you entertained. With friendly locals, a beautiful Andean landscape, and an impressive plaza, Humahuaca is a great place for a day trip.

THINGS TO KNOW

- There are some great places to eat along Buenos Aires Avenue. Be sure to ask a local which one they recommend.

- Fiesta de la Quebrada takes place in February and the town comes alive. Locals wear native costumes and party for a solid week.

THINGS TO DO

Peñas Blancas
An easy 2 km. hike along the Rio Grande that affords a great panoramic view of Quebrada de Humahuaca as well as access to several archaeological sites. To get there from Plaza Central,

take Jujuy Street for two blocks heading north. Turn right onto Salta Street, pass by the craft fair, and cross the bridge over the river Grande. Follow the signs from here.

Monumento a los Héroes de la Independencia

An impressive staircase, which is immediately visible once you enter Plaza Central, leads up to the 70-ton bronze monument, sculpted in honor of the Northern Argentinean Army. Artisans selling their crafts line the stairs as you walk up, and once you reach the top you will see the remains of a Jesuit chapel and a great view of the city.

Museo Arqueológico Municipal

An archaeological museum that holds an impressive collection of Incan mummies and artifacts collected from the northern region of Argentina. To get there, you'll see a sign on the left-hand side of the stairs leading to Monumento a los Héroes de la Independencia.

ACCOMMODATION

Virgen de Agua Chica

Agua Chica was still undergoing construction while we were there, but the upgrades looked exciting. Air-conditioning units were being placed in each room and a terrace with an amazing view of the city was being upgraded. The rooms are clean and most of them have great views. There is also an enormous kitchen upstairs with panoramic windows. Out of all the hostels we visited, due to the location and secure entrance, Agua Chica felt the most tranquil. The downside was the lack of Wi-Fi, but the owners hope to have this fixed in the next year.

Cost: 45–120 pesos
Antártida 378, Humahuaca
+54 (0388) 742-7029

Bella Vista

Bella Vista is just across the bridge from town, along the Rio Grande. They have a large section of land dedicated to camping, as well as a small building with a few shared rooms for rent. As it is a bit off the beaten path, we would only recommend staying here if you have a travel buddy and are prepared to rough it a bit. On the upside, the location is quiet and it seems to attract really friendly travelers.

Cost: 20–120 pesos

La Banda, Humahuaca (just across the bridge to the right)
+54 (0387) 715-587-8136

SHOPPING

Crafts Fair

A large fair on Belgrano, just before the river, takes place all week. Here you can purchase peppers, cocoa leaves, spices, tapestries, fresh empanadas, and hundreds of other items.

Talleres de Cerámica

At these clay pottery studios, artisans create pottery from start to finish for viewers. Pots, vases, urns and dishes are all available for purchase.

TUCUMAN

San Miguel de Tucuman (Tucuman for short) is the capital of one of the most densely populated provinces in Argentina, making it an urban city with few calm, quiet areas. However, this does make for a pretty lively nightlife; there are plenty of clubs, bars and restaurants. It's not on the top of our list of places to spend a night, but if you find yourself here for some reason, here's how to make the best of it.

THINGS TO KNOW

- If you book a hostel near the center, it will be loud through most of the night, so if you're not joining in on the fun, it's smart to book a hostel off the beaten path.

- Walking the streets alone at night is not the best idea. Take a cheap cab if you feel like venturing out to a club, and be sure to drink responsibly.

- The summers here are hot and humid, even unbearably so. If you can find accommodation with air-conditioning, take it even if it costs a little extra; it'll be worth it to get a good night's sleep.

- The men here really kick it up a notch with the catcalls, so don't be surprised to receive even more attention than usual. Best way to cope? Ignore, ignore, ignore. Eyes forward and walk with purpose.

THINGS TO DO

El Cerro San Javier
About 15 miles out of town, San Javier offers a nice escape from the city. Temperatures are cooler at this altitude, and there are several parks, trekking opportunities and even paragliding. Catch a minibus from Tucuman, or arrange an excursion.

ACCOMMODATION

Oh! Hostel
This hostel is in an older building, but was recently renovated. The rooms are clean and fairly spacious, and there is a large female-only locker-room style bathroom upstairs. The common rooms are cozy and the location is set away from the busiest part of town, making it quieter than many of the other hostels. There is also a back patio complete with a grill, bar and small pool. There is a secure entrance monitored by 24-hour staff, and breakfast and Wi-Fi are included. This is your best bet for accommodation in Tucuman.

Cost: 55–75 pesos

Santa Fe 930, San Miguel Tucuman
+54 (0381) 430 8849
contacto@hosteloh.com.ar
www.hosteloh.com.ar

SHOPPING

If you're hoping to shop, Tucuman is not your best bet. While there are small shops and a local market, there's nothing really here that caught our attention. Save your pennies and splurge in Salta.

PATAGONIA

Known around the world for its unique landscapes and incredible outdoor opportunities, Patagonia is a vast and diverse landscape that offers a little something for everyone.

Mountain lakes and jagged peaks with breathtaking views? Check. Rumbling glaciers and sub-zero bars? Check? Beautiful beaches and exotic marine life? Check. Artisan chocolate, ice cream, and beer? Check, check, check.

From the borders of Rio Colorado to the southern tip of the world in Tierra del Fuego, Patagonia spans more than 1,000 miles from north to south, and the endless opportunities for adventure are as diverse as the landscape itself. Whether you've come here to trek, or you're hoping just to relax and take it all in, Patagonia is unlike any other area on Earth.

There are five provinces that make up the region of Patagonia:

- Rio Negro

- Chubut

- Neuquén

- Santa Cruz

- Tierra del Fuego

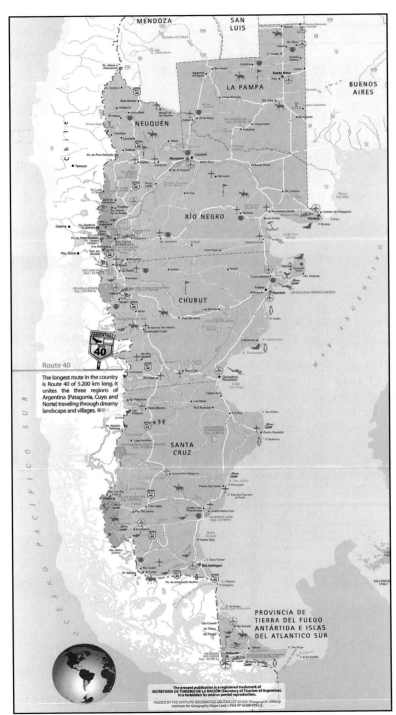

Route 40

The longest route in the country is Route 40 of 5.200 km long. It unites the three regions of Argentina (Patagonia, Cuyo and Norte) traveling through dreamy landscape and villages.

TOP ⭐ PICKS

Best Place to Walk on a Glacier:
Perito Moreno
The sound of the ice rumbling and cracking and creaking alone makes this trip well worth it. Hang out a bit and if you're lucky, you'll get to watch a chunk of ice tumble into the Antarctic waters.

Best Place to Get Lost for a Few Days:
El Bolson
Magic comes up over and over again when travelers describe their time in Bolson. Could be the amazing river or the mountains or the fallen forest. Head there yourself to find out why.

Best Place to Watch Whales:
Puerto Madryn
Watching orcas beach themselves to hunt seals is one of those, once-in-a-lifetime kind of experiences. It's slightly morbid, but also really amazing.

Scenery along Ruta 40

DRIVING DOWN LEGENDARY RUTA 40

Route 40 is the backbone of Argentina, stretching from the border with Bolivia all the way to Ushuaia. Voted one of National Geographic's top 10 drives, it extends nearly 5,000 km. from north to south, and at times reaches altitudes of nearly 5,000 m. It also partially follows El Camino del Inca, a trade route built by the Inca in the 15th century.

Ruta 40 passes through 20 reserves and national parks, 5 UNESCO World Heritage Sites and more than 200 rivers. Whether you rent a car, hitchhike or hop on a tour, jumping on Argentina's oldest highway, now in its 76th year, is a great way to see lots of what the country has to offer.

Tips for the Journey

- To rent a car in Argentina, you must be at least 21 years of age, and have an international driver's license. A couple of companies to check out are Avis, Hertz, Alamo, y Dollar Rent-a-Car. Depending on where you pick up, what type of car, etc. prices range from about 250 – 400 pesos/day. For rentals longer than 1 week, there are generally significant discounts, so be sure to ask.

- Drivers in Argentina are slightly more aggressive than in the U.S. Depending on where you are, make sure to follow local customs. Also, the more stuff you cram in the car, the more attractive it is to thieves. Make sure to always keep your valuables with you, and try to park in areas that are well lit.

- Much of Ruta 40 in Patagonia is unpaved. Get rental car insurance, and drive carefully!

- Stop and fill up every time you see a gas station. It doesn't matter if you're still ¾ full. In certain parts of Ruta 40, especially in Patagonia, petrol stations are few and far between and it may be another few hundred kilometers before you can have another opportunity.

SAN CARLOS DE BARILOCHE

Described as tranquilo by travelers and locals alike, this mountain gem is a must for any visit to southern Patagonia. Known for its incredible hiking, biking, chocolate, ice cream and beer, it's hard to go wrong here. If you're not the cold-weather type, we recommend a summer (November–February) visit, but the town is incredibly beautiful year-round. Boasting a mix of serious climbers and bikers, as well as a handful of hungry backpackers in this Swiss-town, there are parks to relax in, bars to hang out in and people to meet wherever you go. High season is in the summer, December–February, and prices usually go up at least 8 pesos for accommodation, and as much as 20–40 for tours.

HOW TO GET THERE

There are a number of buses that run from Buenos Aires to Bariloche, all of which run around the same price. Via Bariloche and Chevallier buses came most highly recommended, and we hear you can sometimes win a bottle of wine playing late-night bingo on the Andesmar bus.

A ticket to Bariloche costs between 610 and 720 pesos,

depending on whether you choose *cama* or *semi-cama*—the difference between seats that fold all the way back and ones that just recline—and includes all meals. We recommend the overnight bus to ensure you make the most of your time in Bariloche. Buses leave regularly from BA, and arrive nearly 24 hours later. You can usually buy your ticket at the station, but during peak season it isn't a bad idea to book in advance. Check out our favorite site, *www.platforma10.com*, to book your ticket and see what companies depart at what time. Also, your big bag is stored down below the bus, so be sure to bring everything valuable and those things that you may want access to in a small bag you can carry on.

For vegetarians: bring some snacks. There are definitely vegetarian sides with all of the meals, but the main course always had meat.

When you arrive in Bariloche, stop at the information desk for maps and tips, and buy a ticket for the bus that heads to the center. If you get off at Centro Civico, there are at least six hostels within a two-block radius of the square.

THINGS TO KNOW

- Bariloche is a major hub for people visiting from Chile and those headed both north and south, so be sure to take advantage of this opportunity to network.

- There are a number of *refugios*, or small guesthouses, outside of town that offer camping and rustic accommodation. Most of them cost about the same as a hostel. The accommodation is rustic and usually you need to have your own sleeping bag. These mountain hideouts offer an escape outside the city, and easy access to some of the best hikes in the area. El Refugio Emilio Frey is highly recommended.

- You have to buy local bus tickets in advance and cannot buy them on the bus. Most hostels offer the use of their bus card, which you can preload with however many rides you may need for the day at most kiosks. While it is possible to buy tickets in kiosks, using one of these cards will save you about 4 pesos per ride. It may not sound like much, but it can add up.

- A small market sets up on the weekends in the main park in town.

You'll be able to find some really neat jewelry and handicrafts, but you'll have to bargain.

Seasons
Go depending on what you want to do. If you're there for the skiing, July and August are the best months for a visit. For hiking and climbing, the weather is more conducive from late spring to early fall, roughly October–April. We recommend spring and fall for mild climates that allow access to everything the region has to offer. The colors in the fall are unmatched!

Stock Up
If you are heading south from Bariloche, stock up on necessities, as it's the cheapest in the region for essential items like tampons, which become more expensive and harder to find in smaller towns.

THINGS TO DO

Cerrado Campanario
For the best views in the city and a great hike, hop on bus 20 from Centro Civico heading north. The ride takes about 20 minutes, and snakes you through much of Bariloche right on the water. Tell the bus driver where you are headed, and he'll let you know when you reach the stop. Once you arrive, you have two options for reaching the viewpoint: hiking or riding the lift. The hike up is steep and takes 30–40 minutes. The lift takes about 15 minutes, and costs 25 pesos. This is an incredible spot for sunset—consider packing mate and some snacks and parking yourself here to watch.

Colonia Suiza
For arts and crafts in a small Swiss colony, head to Colonia Suiza. From Centro Civico, take the 20 bus heading north as if you were heading to Cerrado Companario. One stop after Cerrado Companario, the 20 will drop you at a big intersection. You can catch the No.10 bus heading to Colonia Suiza from here, but keep in mind that it only departs in the afternoon. Hitchhiking to Colonia Suiza from this intersection is also an option, but works best if you are traveling in a group of one or two. On Wednesdays and Saturdays you can find an art fair here. And, if you do, make sure to visit El Gringo (just ask around) and sample some of his delicious food. While in Colonia Suiza, consider a short walk down

to the lake or a walk up to the mirador for some incredible views.

Ride it Out: For a great way to catch both of the above, consider renting a bike from the intersection where the 20 drops you off or from the stop at Cerrado Companario. Bike rentals cost about 90 pesos for the day, but they're quality bikes. You can then ride to Colonia Suiza, catch the art fair, and continue in a circle, hopping off for some short jaunts through national parks on the water before finishing your ride at Cerrado Companero for sunset. For beginner riders, the ride takes about 3–5 hours. There are some good climbs, and it's best if you've had some experience riding a bike (changing gears and such) before attempting this option.

Cascada de los Duendes
While there are a million things to do and places to get great views in Bariloche, these waterfalls are a bit off the beaten track. The falls are also on the way to El Refugio Emilio Frey, and you could conquer both in one day, or hit the falls on your way to spend a night at the Refugio. Jump the 50 bus from town and tell the driver you are heading to Cascada de los Duendes. He'll drop you off on a dirt road, and from there you will walk about 30 minutes on the dirt road that winds along the lakeshore to the park entrance. From the park entrance, follow the signs for about 20 minutes to get to the falls. There is also a place to rent kayaks at the point when you turn from the road onto the trail.

Ventisquero Negro
The black glacier, aptly named for the ashen color it boasts, is a great place for hiking. This hike came highly recommended as a local favorite, and it isn't very demanding. There are not public buses from town, and it is easiest to have the hostel book your trip with one of the guide companies. They'll usually pick you up around 9 a.m., and a tour costs 150–250 pesos depending on the season and any available promotions (ask), but does not include the park entrance fee of 50 pesos.

············ ACCOMMODATION ············

Bariloche Backpackers Hostel
This hostel is great for a number of reasons, but primarily the location, owner, and the all- female dorm and private bathroom. They have Wi-Fi, a kitchen, a computer and various books and games, and breakfast is included.

The owner doesn't just hand you a map; he sits down and shows you all the best things to do on the cheap. He's lived in Bariloche for some time, and also spent some time in the U.S. so he speaks English. If you're planning on trekking, this is a great place to get tips and to meet up with other travelers headed to the mountains.

Cost: 50–65 pesos for a dorm, and 150–185 pesos for the private room (there is only one).

From the bus station where your bus from Buenos Aires leaves you, you can buy a ticket for the 20 or 21 for 8 pesos, and get off at the central plaza. Backpackers Hostel is across the street and about 20 feet to your right if you get off the bus and head away from the park.

San Martin 82
+54 (0294) 442-8683
info@barilochebackpackers.com
www.barilochebackpackers.com

Penthouse 1004

Located on the top floor of the tallest building in town, this hostel is in our top picks—and the view is just the beginning. Run by a group of friends from Bariloche, everyone is friendly and knowledgeable in this 16-year-old hostel. The place seems to attract an eclectic crowd, and has a number of great community spaces, a clean and full-stocked kitchen, balcony seating and spotless,

comfortable mixed–gender dorms.

Cost: 70–100 pesos for a dorm and 170–200 pesos for a private room, depending on season.

From the bus station where your bus from Buenos Aires leaves you, you can buy a ticket for the 20 or 21 for 8 pesos, and get off at the central plaza. Head to the top of the tallest building on the south side of the park and you'll find the Penthouse 1004 at the end of the hall.

San Martin 127 – Bariloche Center Building
10th floor, Apartment 1004
+54 (0194) 443-2228
penthouse1004@yahoo.com.ar
www.penthouse1004.com.ar

Las Moiras Hostel

Las Moiras Hostel is also conveniently located next to the Civic Center. All rooms, dorms included, have private bathrooms, and there is a great sitting room. Breakfast, Wi-Fi, and the use of a well-stocked kitchen are all included in the price, and some of the rooms offer spectacular views of the water.

Cost: 50–65 pesos for a dorm, and 140–170 pesos for the private rooms.

From the Civic Center, head toward the water on Morales Street for about three blocks. The street winds a little, but you'll be forced to take a right on Reconquista, where the hostel is located about a half block down the way.

Reconquista 72
+54 (0294) 442-7883
info@lasmoiras.com
www.lasmoiras.com

SHOPPING

For Ice Cream and Chocolate

There are a lot of chocolate and ice cream shops in Bariloche, and it's hard to say which are the best. Some of our favorites are Mama Goye and Mamuska, but you should probably try a few for yourself and decide. From the El Centro Civico, you can wander in just about any direction and run into a shop, but most of them are located close to the water.

Ice cream in Bariloche

For Handicrafts

In Colonia Suiza, there is an arts fair on Wednesdays and Saturdays from 10 a.m. until about 6 p.m. Keep in mind that the buses to Colonial Switzerland don't head up to the village until about 10 a.m. Take bus 20 out of town toward Cerro Campanario and get off one stop after the stop for the vista. Then, catch the 10. If you're early, you can try hitchhiking, but there are few cars early in the morning. There is also a small market that sets up on the weekends in the Central Plaza.

NEUQUÉN

With a population of nearly 300,000, Neuquén is the capital of the Neuquén province of Argentina, and the largest city in Patagonia. Originally an industrial center (primarily for drilling and processing oil), Neuquén is gaining more and more ground as a tourist destination. It is a pretty city, with many tree-lined streets and parks—many of which house beautiful multiple sculptures, museums, and easy access to a wide range of great outdoor activities. Of late, Neuquén is being touted as one of the best fly-fishing spots in the world.

HOW TO GET THERE

Buses leave from Buenos Aires for Neuquén up to 20 times a day and cost between 450–600 pesos. The ride is approximately 18 hours, and all buses headed toward Bariloche and other popular Patagonian cities pass through here. A one-way flight on LAN from Buenos Aires runs about 800 pesos. *www.lan.com.ar*.

THINGS TO KNOW

Tourism is definitely not Neuquén's main industry, and they're still working out the kinks. You will not find the same quality or diversity of accommodation and tours that you might find in Bariloche or El Calafate, where tourism is the industry.

THINGS TO DO

Avenida Argentina and the Balcony of the Valley
The main street in Neuquén is Avenida Argentina. Wandering down the avenue, you'll find a number of parks full of sculptures, fountains and galleries. There is a plaza of flags, and on one side of the plaza a lookout—Balcony of the Valley—from which you have some great views of the entire city. On a clear day, you can see the convergence of the Neuquén and Limay Rivers into Rió Negro.

Dinosaurs
Known as one of the richest paleontological sites in South America, Neuquén offers a number of ways to experience the history of

the region. El Museo Paleontológico Municipal Ernesto Bachman is open from 8 a.m. to 7 p.m. every day, and for 8 pesos you can spend the day checking out fossils, skeletons and exhibits and learning more about the rich history of the region. Don't forget to check out the tracks outside the museum—it's super cool!

Acceso Centro al Cívico 8311
+54 299-490-1230/ 1223

Wine

Neuquén is gaining a name for itself in the wine scene. The region boasts distinct flavors produced by its relatively cool climate. Most of the wineries are in the east, anywhere from 20 km. to 130 km. outside of Neuquén and the most common types of wines produced are Cabernet Sauvignon, Malbec, Merlot, Pinot Noir, Chardonnay, Sauvignon Blanc and Semillon. Wine tours cost 200 pesos and up. Vinoteca La Barrica offers different tour options.

Vinoteca La Barrica
Calle Roca 421
+54 (0299) 442-2397
contacto@labarricanqn.com.ar

········· **ACCOMMODATION** ·········

De Paso Hostel

This house converted into a hostel provides a comfortable place to crash during your time in Neuquén. There is a nice terrace with a parrilla, and the kitchen is very open, making it easy to cook while talking to new friends, and we're always fans of that. Breakfast is included. One thing to note: if you choose to book in advance, this hostel has a 72-hour cancellation policy.

Cost: The price for a six-bed mixed dorm is 80 pesos, and prices go up to 450 pesos for a private room.

If you arrive in the bus station located on 12 de Septiembre, the hostel is about 2 km. or 16 blocks. If you're up for the walk, head east on General San Jose de Martin eight blocks, and then turn left on Chrestia Garcia for seven blocks. Take a right when you get to Sargento Cabral for half a block and the hostel will be on your left. If you're not up for the walk, hop in a taxi for around 18 pesos.

Sargento Cabral 975
+54 (0299) 442-3620
info@depasohostel.com
www.depasohostel.com.ar

Hostel Portal de Sueños

The ping-pong table and pool are just a few of the things this hostel has going for it. The staff is really friendly and informed, and can help organized tours from within the hostel or with partner organizations. The breakfast, the cost of which is included in the prices, includes cereal and yogurt in addition to the standard bread and dulce de leche, and the backyard is a nice gathering place for cookouts and games.

Cost: 70 pesos for a dorm, 110 for a private room and bathroom. Private, secured parking is 20 pesos.

This hostel is just four blocks from the bus station. Walk east two blocks on General Jose de San Martin and take a left on Colonel Rufino Ortega. Walk two more blocks to the intersection with Pilar and turn right. The hostel will be one and a half blocks down on your left.

Pilar 3257
+54 (0299) 446-7643
info@hostelportal.com.ar
www.hostelportal.net

SHOPPING

Feria de Neuquén

If you find yourself in Neuquén over the weekend, be sure to stop by this fair for some of the best crafts in the area. The fair got its start in the late '80s and is now full of nearly 170 craftsmen and performers each weekend. In the fair you will find many of the same things that you can find further down the road in Bariloche and Calafate—silver, ceramics, leather, etc.—but for slightly less. Prices go up 10 or more pesos for most things in more touristy cities. The fair is open every Friday, Saturday and Sunday, as well as on holidays.

Avenida Argentina 200

EL BOLSON

El Bolson is a small artist's community set between Bariloche and El Calafate, but it's certainly a destination worth a visit all on its own. While there are a number of great restaurants and shops in town, the real magic is in the mountains, rivers and lakes surrounding the place. The hikes around the area are unmatched.

HOW TO GET THERE

There are a number of buses that pass through El Bolson, but the only one that comes straight from Bariloche is Via Bariloche. Andesmar and Chevallier pass through. You can buy the ticket for El Bolson for about 50 pesos at the bus station in Bariloche, or at one of two Via Bariloche ticket offices located near the center of town.

THINGS TO KNOW

- The artist community here is very active and present. There is an arts fair in the main square Monday, Wednesday, Saturday and Sunday, and it draws a healthy crowd.

- Hitchhiking in and around El Bolson is very common and accepted. Many of the hikes are not accessible by bus, and so aside from renting a car or going in a taxi, hitchhiking is sometimes the only option.

- If we had to recommend one place to stay in a refugio, this would probably be it. There are a number, but two of the most highly recommended are El Refugio Hielo Azul and El Refugio Piltriquitron.

- The information center located in the middle of town in the city square has tons of information and the people working there are very helpful.

- If you are interested in WOOFing, there are a number of farms in El Bolson. While we can't recommend any one specifically, this would be a great place to start your process and to be guaranteed a beautiful work environment with a very conscientious community. Small, organic farms are plentiful, and it's still the kind of place you can wander to a neighbor's house to buy fresh milk and vegetables.

THINGS TO DO

Lago Puelo

For 20 pesos you can take a 45-minute bus ride from town to Lago Puelo for some incredible views—and, depending on the time of the year, kayaking or swimming. If you walk for about 20 minutes down the road from the bus stop, you will find yourself at the Lakes Shores, where you can picnic, swim, rent kayaks, or head up the mountain to a viewpoint on the way to Cerro Plataforma Refugio.

El Bosque Tallado and Refugio Piltriquitron

The Fallen Forest is a must-see in El Bolson. This high-elevation forest is an almost surreal experience. Local artists have turned what were a number of fallen trees into beautiful sculptures gracing the mountainside. El Bosque Tallado is about a 700-meter or 30-minute walk from the parking lot, and it's easy to spend close to an hour wandering the forest and finding all of the hidden gems. If you carry on the same trail for about another 10 minutes, you reach El Refugio Piltriquitron, which offers incredible views as well. Stay for 40 pesos and climb some of the nearby peaks early the next morning before heading down. Fall was an incredible time for this hike as the colors at this altitude were unreal—so vibrant!

El Hielo Azul

Originally constructed in 1958, El Hielo Azul is a trek with two to three peaks for you to explore, and a refugio to spend the night in, should you choose to. Access requires crossing the Rio Azul, which is exceptionally beautiful. The hike is free, and stay at the refugio costs around 40 pesos. If you intend to climb one of the peaks, it is recommended that you use one day to hike the refugio (don't forget to take a peek at the stars), and then wake early to climb and return to town the next day.

ACCOMMODATION

Altos del Sur

This lovely hostel is definitely off the beaten track, but then, that's sort of the beauty of it. Located at the base of the walk to El Bosque Tallado and Piltriquitron, this is a perfect base-point for further exploration. The women who run the place live nearby, and they keep it in pristine condition. Clean and warm, this is more like a cabin get-away than a hostel. The grounds also offer fireplaces and amazing viewpoints where you can see El Bolson and the surrounding mountains. There is a grill and a huge, open, and fully stocked kitchen. This place is definitely worth the trek.

Cost: 60–70 pesos for a dorm, 160–180 pesos, for a private room, or rent a private cabin with four beds for 230–260 pesos.

From the center, you can take a taxi all the way there. Or, take a taxi or bus to where the dirt road to Piltriquitron begins. No one seems to know the name of the road, so it's best just to ask for Piltriquitron. From there you will see signs leading to the hostel. It's about a 30-minute walk up the dirt road.

3 Cipreses N 1237
+54 (0294) 449-8730
www.altosdelsur.bolsonweb.com

La Casa del Arbol

Just blocks from the city center, La Casa del Arbol, also known as Hostel El Bolson, offers a comfy and casual home away from home. A fireplace in the central room keeps the place warm, and the kitchen is massive and fully equipped. A back yard barbecue is available for guests to make their own asado while playing ping-pong and hanging out in the hammocks that grace the yard. They have off-street parking for those traveling by car, and offer a range of accommodation. Breakfast and Wi-Fi are included.

Cost: 50-150 pesos

Continue heading north on San Martin from the information *center and take a right on Calle Azcuenaga. Hang a left around the roundabout and the hostel will be right there, just a block and a half off of San Martin.*

Perito Moreno 3038
+54 (0294) 472-0176
contacto@hostelelbolson.com
www.hostelelbolson.com

SHOPPING

El Bolson is the place for hand-made arts and crafts, and if you haven't yet picked up a mate cup, here's the place for it! Cheaper than both Bariloche and El Calafate, there are a number of arts and crafts stores along the main street, as well on the country roads outside of town.

Arts Fair
As we said earlier, the artist community here rocks. You can't miss their arts fair, held in the main square Monday, Wednesday, Saturday and Sunday.

Almerco
El Bolson also has two rather large Almerco supermarkets that offer anything and everything for a reasonable price—definitely cheaper than Calafate, so stock up here before heading south, especially on vegetables and personal items.

Lago Epuyen

LAGO EPUYEN AND TREVELIN

Both Lago Epuyen and the nearby picturesque town of Trevelin, a small Welsh settlement, are peaceful escapes from the city life that both tourists and Argentine natives take advantage of. While there are options year-round, summer and fall are considered the most accessible and beautiful times for a visit. Consider taking a few days' reprieve from your trip in these beautiful spots.

HOW TO GET THERE

You can get to Lago Epuyen or Trevelin from Bariloche, or by hitchhiking or busing from El Bolson. If you are coming up from the south, you can catch a bus from Esquel to Lago Epuyen. Most of the camping spots and cabanas are about a 30-45 minute walk outside of town. Because things differ so significantly between the seasons, we recommend asking around in El Bolson before you make the trip to Lago Epuyen and consider making a reservation before you go. Depending on the season, accommodation can cost anywhere from 40 to 250 pesos. If you're traveling with a group, consider renting a cabana to cut costs, and ask around to find out the most affordable options.

THINGS TO KNOW

- Hostels are not open year-round, but there are always camping options.

- Whether hitchhiking or busing from Bolson further south, Lago Epuyen is a beautiful and relaxing place to rejuvenate before heading further south.

THINGS TO DO

El Parque Nacional Los Alceres
There are a number of hikes in the forests nearby and a visit to El Parque Nacional Los Alerces is a must. Visit some of the oldest trees on Earth while you wander the woods around nine different lakes. Spend a couple of days in this enchanted forest by camping in the mini-settlement Villa Fatalaufquen, located inside the park.

Go Skiing

Most of the refugios and campsites along the lake offer boat rentals, guided tours, and fishing. In the winter, some of them offer skiing. Most activities cost 100–300 pesos, depending on the activity and the duration.

Visit Welsh Settlements

Trevelin is the launching point for a number of excursions to visit the Welsh and Mapuche Indian cultures that have roots in the region.

·········· **ACCOMMODATION** ··········

Trevelin
Casaverde Hostel

Casaverde is a beautiful cabin nestled along the shores of the river. The massive garden is a picturesque place to relax in a hammock and enjoy the trees, flowers, birds and more. The common spaces are bright and open, and there's a small cabin out back that you can rent for special events. Price includes towels, and there are male, female and mixed dorms. This hostel is closed at random points throughout the year, so it is definitely worth calling or emailing in advance to make your reservation.

Cost: 60-70 pesos

Located four blocks from the main plaza on Los Alerces, this hostel is really easy to find. Depending on how you arrive, it is easiest just to ask.

Los Alerces s/n
+54 (294) 548-0091
casaverdehostel@infovia.com.ar

Lago Epuyen
El Refugio del Lago

More than just a hostel, this refugio offers camping and cabanas for 2-4 people for reasonable prices that include breakfast and linens (in the cabanas). With beach access, canoe rentals on site, volleyball courts and ping-pong tables, this place is perfect for a couple of tranquil days on the shores of Lago Epuyen.

Cost: 50 pesos for space in a small cabana

Located a bit outside of town on Los Alerces (there is no specific address), it is easiest just to ask from where you land. If you are in town center, hitchhiking is an option. Just ask the locals— they'll get you there!

Los Alerces s/n
+54 (0294) 549-9025
a.sophie@epuyen.net.ar
www.elrefugiodellago.com.ar

There are some small shops in Trevelin, but there's not much to shop for. Take a break from spending money and just enjoy the natural scenery. If you do need something, shop in nearby El Bolson, or stock up before you head towards Lago Epuyen, Trevelin, or other small communities nearby.

ESQUEL

Esquel is considered a strategic and scenic stopping point on route between San Carlos de Bariloche or El Bolson and El Calafate, but the town offers some attractions of its own. Though travelers seem to have mixed reviews of the city itself, nearby Los Alerces National Park is a must-see for outdoor enthusiasts and the historic La Trochita Railway is a unique way to travel between Esquel and the small mountain town of Ingeniero Jacobacci.

····················· **HOW TO GET THERE** ·····················

You can travel to Esquel straight from Buenos Aires via bus for about 700 pesos or from San Carlos de Bariloche for about 80 pesos. The ride from Buenos Aires is about 30 hours, and from Bariloche it is about seven hours. You can also take a bus from El Bolson for about 60 pesos, which takes three to four hours. Hitchhiking anywhere from Bariloche to Esquel is common and simple, but always use your best judgment. Allow yourself a bit of extra time, and be sure to ask where you will be getting dropped off when you are picked up to ensure there is accommodation in that area.

····················· **THINGS TO KNOW** ·····················

Esquel is a major stopping point on the way to El Calafate, and most buses leave from Esquel around 1 p.m. and head through Rio Gallegos to El Calafate for a 27-hour bus ride that costs about 660 pesos.

You can fly from Esquel to Rio Gallegos and catch a bus from there (only four hours), and in high season you have the option of flying directly to El Calafate. Prices vary, but can be found online and are generally around 1,000 pesos.

Los Alerces National Park

Take a boat trip to this 3,000-year-old forest, where some of the trees are more than 200 feet tall. It's a bit of a trek to get here, so consider camping at Lago Verde or one of the other campsites and allow yourself two to three days to play in the forest and the nearby peaks. Park entrance costs 30 pesos, and most activities in the park (boat rides, etc.) are less than 100 pesos.

La Trochita Train Ride

A must for train enthusiasts, a ride on the Old Patagonian Express provides incredible panoramic views of the area and a wealth of information about the area's natural landscapes and rich cultural history. The track is lovingly named La Trochita for the small width of the tracks—only 29.5 inches wide. Prices vary drastically depending on the time of year, type of trip, and number of other passengers so it's best to inquire at the La Roca train station in El Centro.

ACCOMMODATION

Caso del Pueblo

This 40-year-old hostel offers travelers a fun, comfortable place to stay with all the bells and whistles, like homemade bread for breakfast, Wi-Fi, lockers, and trip planning services from staff that speak Spanish, English, and German. The kitchen is fully stocked with anything you could ever need.

Cost: 60–70 pesos for a dorm, 100–120 pesos for a double.

From the bus terminal, follow Avenida Alvear for 11 blocks and then take a left on Bartolome Mitre. Go three blocks and take a right on San Martin, where you will find the hostel on the left side.

San Martin 661
+54 (0294) 545-0481
hostelcasadelpueblo@hotmail.com
www.hostelcasadelpueblo.com.ar

Planeta Hostel

Planeta Hostel has it all, and it's very close to the bus station. There are a number of great things about this place, but the kitchen and indoor climbing wall were some of our favorites. The owners are very friendly and offer great advice on all things to do in the mountains, especially climbing and mountain biking.

Cost: 60–100 pesos

Stay on Avenido Alvear heading toward town. Take a left on General Roca and the hostel will be three blocks down. If you hit Avenido Ameghino, you've gone too far.

General Roca 458
+54 (0294) 545-6846
contacto@planetahostel.com
www.planetahostel.com

EL CHALTEN

Located at the base of one of the world's most technically challenging mountains to climb—Monte Fitz Roy—El Chalten is an idealistic mountain village located three hours outside of El Calafate. The town and mountains surrounding it offer some of the most incredible views the region has to offer, and world-renowned climbing opportunities of Monte Fitz Roy and Cerro Torre.

In the summer the little town is bustling and in the winter it's nearly abandoned, but the views of the glaciers in the southern part of Parque Nacional de Los Glaciares, Lago del Desierto and Fitz Roy are worth the trip any time of year. It's a town that attracts both the most intense and technical mountaineers and more tranquil lovers of mountain vistas.

HOW TO GET THERE

From El Calafate, buses leave fairly regularly for El Chalten depending on the season and cost between 100–150 pesos. Transport from anywhere will pass through El Calafate, but it is possible to purchase your ticket from various locations in Argentina straight through to El Chalten. If El Chalten is your main attraction, consider flying to El Calafate (accessible from Buenos Aires and Ushuaia year-round) and catching the bus from there.

Heads Up: In winter, we highly advise booking your tickets in advance as trips are sparse and can fill up randomly with student groups on vacation. There's only one company, so it can be pretty easy to get stranded.

THINGS TO DO

Trekking, trekking, trekking. There are a huge number of options for climbing mountains in and around El Chalten. Your best bet is to talk to people—both at hostels and tour companies—while you are there to find out what is accessible, best for the weather and what matches your abilities. From beautiful mountain lakes to steep mountain peaks, El Chalten offers a range for all seasons and all abilities. Most locations are accessible both via guided and unguided tours. Should you choose the unguided route, be sure to check in with locals to ascertain trail and or road conditions.

Mount Fitz Roy
At 3,405 meters, this beast of a mountain is incredible to look at and even more rewarding to climb. While this is one of the most technical mountains in the world, there are also options for shorter, easier hikes and a range of options for climbing the granite walls of the mountain.

El Lago del Desierto
This incredible lake is a 32-km. drive up a rustic dirt road, and then a 200-meter hike to the shore. The lake is surrounded by glaciers, and appears to almost fold off of the mountain into them. There are a number of trails and vistas around the shore, and in the summer a nearby restaurant and refugio offer both pizza and accommodation.

ACCOMMODATION

Albergue Patagonia

Albergue Patagonia Travelers' Hostel is located in the heart of El Chalten on Avenue San Martin, 300 meters from the beginning of all the trails to El Parque Nacional de Los Glaciales. The hostel has been offering accommodation for nearly 18 years, and last year underwent a major remodel. Everything is new and clean, breakfast is included, and there is a restaurant on site. Wi-Fi and central heating are some additional perks. Alberque Patagonia is also the only hostel that organizes mountain bike tours to Lago del Desierto.

Cost: 70–90 pesos

If you get dropped off at Rancho Grande Hostel, walk about three blocks on the main road toward the center of town and the hostel will be on your right. If you get dropped off at the bus station, walk the opposite direction on the main road, back toward the center of town for about four blocks; the hostel will be on your left. El Chalten is really very small, so you can't miss it!

Avenida San Martin 493
El Chalten
+54 (0296) 249-3019
patagoniahostel@yahoo.com.ar
www.patagoniahostel.com.ar

Rancho Grande Hostel

This hostel has been around longer than most others in El Chalten, and is also open year-round. With a big family room and a perfect table to gather around, this place offers a great space for sharing stories from the day. Breakfast is not included, but Wi-Fi is.

Cost: 70–85 pesos

Odds are that you will either be dropped off here or at the bus station. Either way, Rancho Grande is located on the main strip on the east end of town. It's impossible to miss, but if you ask around, anyone and everyone can tell you where it is.

Avenue San Martin 724
ranchogrande@chaltentravel.com
www.ranchograndehostel.com

SHOPPING

If you're looking for camping, hiking, or trekking gear, you'll find it in El Chalten along the main road.

EL CALAFATE

El Calafate is probably best known as the jumping-off point for Los Glaciares National Park, but the city is beautiful and entertaining in and of itself. Named for a local berry-producing bush, El Calafate is an important tourist destination, granting access to mountains and glaciers and offering a wide range of hostels, hotels, restaurants and shops. The Glacier Museum in town also includes an ice bar that is a must-see, and if you're into the great outdoors, you're in luck. From two-hour hikes to multi-day ice-climbing adventures, El Calafate has it all.

HOW TO GET THERE

You can get to El Calafate straight from Bariloche on a 28-hour bus ride that costs between 730 and 850 pesos. You can also catch a bus from El Bolson for 700 pesos, Esquel for 700 pesos or Rio Gallegos for 150 pesos. You also have the option to fly to El Calafate, which costs at least 1,540 pesos from Buenos Aires, increasing significantly during the summer months.

El Calafate has an international airport that offers nonstop flights to and from Buenos Aires, Ushuaia, Puerto Madryn, Trelew and Puerto Natales.

- El Calafate is a small town. The main road in town holds most of the action, including Internet cafés, pharmacies, tour operators and hostels.

- Perito Moreno is the main glacier within Los Glaciares National Park. To get there on a budget, try to ride-share with others in your hostel.

- It can get very cold here during the winter months. Summer nights can also be a bit chilly.

THINGS TO DO

Perito Moreno Glacier in Parque a Los Glaciares
This incredible glacier located with Los Glaciares National Park is probably the most popular attraction near El Calafate, and for good reason. It's huge, and the sound of ice cracking and falling into the ocean is unlike any other sound on Earth. The trip to El Perito Moreno from El Calafate costs close to 250 pesos with bus and park entry (100 pesos). A boat ride and/or trek around the berg will cost you anywhere from 300 pesos upwards.

Horse rides/Trekking/Ice-Climbing and Jeep Rides
On the main strip in El Calafate (Avenida del Libertador General San Martin) there are a number of tour companies offering adventure packages. The most affordable option we found offered trekking, horseback riding and jeep tours for 250 pesos. The price went up from there, but so did the type and length of excursion.

Glaciarium – Museo del Hielo Patagonia
Buses leave every hour between 9 a.m. and 6 p.m. from the tourist center on San Martin for this amazing museum. The museum is open from 9 a.m.–8 p.m., and you should allow yourself at least two hours to explore it in full. The bus is 25 pesos, and museum entrance is 80 pesos. You'll want to bring a bit extra and hang out at the GlacioBar. A little expensive, but when else will you have the chance to drink in a below-10 degree Celsius atmosphere, fully dressed in arctic gear? Find out more online at www.glaciarium.com/2012.

ACCOMMODATION

Albergue Lago Argentino

Located just a few blocks up from the center of town and extremely close to the bus stop, this hostel offers an awesome atmosphere in a colorful and serene older building. There are two different segments of the hostel: a traditional-style hostel and then across the street, a series of private rooms in cabins. Both sides are clean, colorful and reasonably priced. The kitchen is large, and the outdoor areas on both sides are beautiful. In addition, and importantly, unlike many hostels in El Calafate, this hostel is open year-round. Breakfast and Wi-Fi are included, and laundry is available for 35 pesos.

Cost: 60–80 pesos for a dorm and 200–240 pesos for a private room.

If you head away from the center one block from the bus station on Avenida Roca, and then take a left of Campana del Desierto you will find the hostel in walking distance from the bus station.

Campana del Desierto 1050
El Calafate
+54 (290) 249-1423
hostellagoargentino@cotecal.
com.ar
www.hostellagoargentino.com.ar

Americana del Sur

This hostel is definitely one of the most popular, largely because the panoramic view offered from the shared space is gorgeous. Located about seven blocks from the bus stop and near the river, this hostel has all the amenities you could want and a welcoming interior. Breakfast is included, as is free transportation from the bus station and room cleaning.

Cost: 60–80 pesos for a dorm and 130–170 pesos for a private room.

Head down the stairs from the bus station and hang a right on Avenida Libertador. After you cross the river, hang a left on Colonel Rosales and then the first right on Puerto San Julian. After two short blocks, you hang another left on Puerto Deseado, and the hostel will be on your right.

Puerto Deseado N 153
El Calafate
+54 (0290) 249-3525
calafate@americahostel.com.ar
www.americahostel.com.ar

Hostel de Las Manos

This hostel is a tranquil option for clean, quiet accommodation and is just seven minutes' walking distance from the bus stop. The rooms are simple but clean and the staff is very kind and helpful. Breakfast and Wi-Fi are included, and the staff is more than happy to store your things and help you plan excursions.

Cost: Dorms are anywhere from 50–70 pesos and private rooms are from 130–150 pesos.

Head down the stairs from the bus stop and walk straight on Avenida 9 de Julio for about six blocks. After about six blocks, the street will come to stop at a bridge. Cross the bridge and hang a left, and then your first right. The hostel will be in the middle of the block on your right.

Calle Egidio Feruglio 59
El Calafate
+54 (0290) 249-2996
hosteldelasmanos@cotecal.com.ar
www.hosteldelasmanos.com.ar

SHOPPING

On the main strip there are a number of shops for all things Patagonia—leather, sweaters, mate, scarves, etc. It takes about 15 minutes to walk from one end to the other, and in the summer the shops are open until 9 p.m. or later. In the winter, however, many of the shops are closed or are only open until about 6 p.m. On the southern end of the main strip there is a supermarket, and all along the strips are banks with ATMs, at least two of which are open 24 hours.

Panaderia Juan Julio
There are a number of great *panaderias*, or bakeries, in El Calafate, but one of our favorites is Panaderia Juan Julio. There are multiple locations, but the one on Calle 9 de Julio has a great atmosphere.

Borges y Alvarez Libro Bar
Pizza shops and bars are also plentiful on the main drag, but one of our favorites is Borges and Alvarez. This bar boasts walls filled with books—many of which are guidebooks for the region—along with a number of great artisan beers and a really fun and friendly staff.

La Guerra Chocolate Shop
You have your pick of chocolate shops on the streets of El Calafate, but one of our favorites is Guerrero Chocolates on the north end of town. The shop has been there for 40 years, and the woman who owns it is friendly and loves it when female travelers come visit her and ask her for recommendations.

RIO GALLEGOS

Though Rio Gallegos is one of the larger cities in Argentina, there is not a whole lot going on—at least not as far as tourism is concerned. It is, however, a major stopping-off point for most people traveling around southern Patagonia (specifically El Calafate, Ushuaia, and Puerto Natales), so it's not a bad idea to have a couple of options in case you get stranded between buses. Most of the travel done in this area is related to business, so accommodation is generally more expensive.

ACCOMMODATION

Keep in mind: Reservations may be hard to make online or over the phone.

Sleepers Inn Hostel
This simple but nice hostel offers breakfast, warm showers, and both dorms and private rooms.

Cost: 80 pesos

Federico Sphur 78 (between Avenida Roca and Alberdi)
+54 (0296) 644-4359

Hotel Cavadonga
Very basic, but conveniently located with reasonably priced rooms.

Cost: 80-120 pesos/person/night.

Avenida Presidente Roca 1244
+54 (0296) 642-0190

THINGS TO DO

Go Fishing
Rio Gallegos is situated on the river, so you can head that way for some decent parks and vistas. If you're in Rio Gallegos, and fishing is your thing, there is a growing trout fishing tourism industry; tours generally run 200 pesos and up.

Visit Cabo Vírgenes to See Penguins
If you happen to be there between October and March, day trips to Cabo V, The large Vírgenes, 140 km. southeast of Río Gallegos, can be booked through Maca Tobiano Turismo. The lighthouse here has been in operation since 1904 and there's plenty of opportunity to see wildlife, including pengins. Tours usually run about 160 pesos, which includes park admission. An eight-hour

trip costs 145 pesos, plus 10 pesos for park admission.

Avenida Roca 998
www.macatobiano.com
+54 (0296) 642-2466

USHUAIA

Commonly referred to as *el fin del mundo* (the end of the world), Ushuaia is the southern-most city in the world. In the late 1800s, the city was founded as a penal colony, housing some of the region's most notorious criminals and political prisoners, inmates who essentially built the town.

Nestled between the Andes and the Beagle Channel, Ushuaia offers a plethora of opportunities for outdoor and cultural exploration. Known both for its strategic naval base and industrial hub as well as its incredible natural landscapes and wildlife, Ushuaia is becoming increasingly attractive to both tourists and Argentines for the job and adventure opportunities it offers.

HOW TO GET THERE

Ushuaia is a trek from just about anywhere, but popular enough that is accessible from a number of locations both in and outside of Argentina. If Tierra del Fuego is your primary target, it's definitely worth the flight. Flights from Buenos Aires run anywhere from about 600 pesos and up, depending on the season and airline. Check LADE *www.lade.com.ar*, LAN *www.lan.com.ar*, or Aerolinas Argentinas *www.aerolineas.com.ar* for flight information.

Buses travel to Ushuaia from just about anywhere in Patagonia, all of them stopping in Rio Gallegos. The bus ride from Buenos Aires to Rio Gallegos is 38 hours and costs approximately 1,100 pesos. From Rio Gallegos to Ushuaia is another 12 hours, and costs approximately 425 pesos. From El Calafate to Ushuaia the ride is approximately 16 hours and costs around 600 pesos.

THINGS TO KNOW

- In the winter (June–August), trips are less regular, and many of the hostels close for random weeks at a time. It is definitely worth booking both transportation and accommodation in advance, especially if you are on a tight schedule.

- Ushuaia is expensive in terms of accommodation, transportation and entertainment. You can cut your costs some by cooking in hostels and going on hikes and other excursions without guides.

- The weather can change quickly in Ushuaia, and when there is wind, it's fierce! Bring your thermals and your wind and waterproof gear.

THINGS TO DO

Museo Maritimi and Museo del Presidio
This museum located near the city center offers a wealth of information on topics ranging from the history of the city to the Antarctic excursions that launch from Ushuaia. Part of the museum is in the original prison building, and some of the rooms remain exactly as they were when the building was abandoned in the 1940s. Entrance is 70 pesos, 40 pesos for students.
9410 Ushuaia between Yaganes y Gobernado Pas

Boat Tour of Beagle Channel

There are a number of companies to choose from for these excursions, and prices range anywhere from about 200 to 500 pesos for the sailing excursion with meals, etc. We recommend going with one of the smaller boats so that you aren't battling lots of people for views of the island. A couple of suggestions: Navegando el Fin del Mundo has two smaller boats, *yate tango* and *yate che*. Unlike some of the larger vessels, they can get a bit closer to the islands, stop at Isla Bridges for a mini-trekking, and have artisan beer on tap inside the boat. This and other boat companies are located on the main doc near the intersection of Avenida 25 de Mayo and Avenida Maipu.
www.navegandoelbeagle.com

El Parque Nacional del Tierra del Fuego

The park, located 11 km. west of Ushuaia, is accessible from the city via bus or taxi ride. The bus, which leaves from Avenida Maipu near the city center, costs about 90 pesos round-trip, and the park entrance is 85 pesos. The park has a number of trails for accessing the beautiful beaches, meandering through the beech forests, and spotting some of the 90 different animal species found within the park. Give yourself at least a day to see the park, or rent a tent (if you don't have one of your own) and take advantage of the camping opportunities within the park.

························· ACCOMMODATION ·························

Antarctica Hostel

This beautiful hostel has a beautiful communal space, a full bar, music, garden spaces, ski storage and a great music selection. The location of the hostel is very central, close to the museum and the bay, and the views of both Beagle Channel and the mountains are added bonuses. While checkout is 10 a.m., the staff at Antarctica Hostel understands life on the road and are very accommodating. They also have all kinds of great hook-ups for local adventures, including dog-sled rides.

Cost: Dorm rooms are 85 pesos and private double rooms are 130 pesos.

From the bus stop, head east on Avenida Maipu approximately seven blocks. Hang a left on Anartida Argentia and walk three more blocks. The hostel will be on your left.

Antartida Argentina 270
+54 (02910) 143-5774

info@antarcticahostel.com
www.antarcticahostel.com

Hostel Patagonia Pais

Starting with Gordita, the pup who acts as hostel mascot, this place is full of character. The staff is incredibly friendly, and by the end of your stay you will definitely feel among friends. The common spaces are conducive for meeting other travelers and the giant kitchen table has hosted many a hostel-dinner amongst newfound friends. They also have bikes for rent and a parrilla out back. Unlike many hostels in Ushuaia, this one is open year-round, and is more affordable than many of the others.

Cost: All rooms are dorms, and beds cost 60 pesos year-round.

Approximately seven minutes walking from the bus station. Head east on Avenida Maipu from the bust station. Hang a left on Yaganes for approximately six blocks. The stay left at the major roundabout intersection. The street changes to Avenida Alem, and about one and a half blocks up the hill you'll find Patagonia Pais on your left.

Avenida Alem 152
+54 (290) 143-1886
patagoniapais@hotmail.com
www.hostelpatagoniapais.com.ar

Los Lupinos Backpackers Hostel

As the largest hostel in Ushuaia, Los Lupinos is a great place for connecting with other travelers, and likely has space in the busy season when things get booked up. The kitchen is large with lots of seating, and can support multiple people cooking at a time. Rooms have great views, and the central location grants easy access to both daytime and nighttime activities Ushuaia has to offer. Breakfast, while basic, is included in the price, and laundry is available on-site.

Cost: Six-person dorms are 85 pesos, and the prices for private rooms range from 230 pesos for a single room with a shared bath to 455 pesos for a four-person room with a private bathroom.

From the bus station, head north two blocks on Avenido 9 de Julio and take a right on Delogui. The hostel will be on your right!

Deloqui 750
+54 (0290) 142-4152
www.loslupinos.com

SHOPPING

As we mentioned before, Ushuaia is expensive so definitely don't plan on stocking up on your everyday necessities here. That said, Ushuaia is a tax-free zone, and so these items are definitely worth checking out there:

Electronics
Cameras and the like are cheaper here because they are manufactured and assembled nearby. There are a number of camera and computer shops on Avenida San Martin.

Alcohol
Liquor is cheap (tax-free) and while it can be found at lots of shops, one of the easiest and cheapest is in the shopping center, La Ultima Bita, located at Avenida San Martin 237. Ultima Bita boasts a range of regional and imported goods and makes a great shopping stop for souvenirs.

Cold-Weather Gear
While not significantly cheaper, you can find name brands like Patagonia and North Face for reasonable prices in a number of stores on Avenida San Martin.

TRELEW

This little Welsh village, named after a Welsh settler arriving to the region—"Tre" means town and "Lew" for Lewis—is often overlooked for its nearby neighbor, Puerto Madryn. Trelew, however is a bit cheaper than Puerto Madryn, boasts a wealth of Welsh heritage, and is located closer to Punta Tombo, which is the largest penguin colony in South America. This sleepy little town doesn't really have much, if anything, to offer to tourists, but maybe that's why you're visiting in the first place.

HOW TO GET THERE

Trelew is located approximately 50 km. from Puerto Madryn and is accessible via bus from Puerto Madryn for 30 pesos. From Buenos Aires, the bus ride is approximately 20 hours and costs 550+ pesos. From Rio Gallegos, the ride is approximately 15 hours for 450+ pesos.

- If you are traveling to Puerto Madryn from Calafate or Ushuaia, you'll pass through Rio Gallegos.

- If your main goal is wildlife, the best time to visit is between September and March. If you visit during the months of May and June, there are very few or potentially no animals around.

························ **THINGS TO DO** ························

Punta Tombo

Punta Tombo is the largest penguin reserve in South America, with nearly 1 million Magellan penguins arriving each year to breed. The nature reserve of Punta Tombo is home to the largest colony of Magellanic penguins in the world. The coolest thing about this park is that when you are there, you're literally walking with the penguins. There are certainly some areas that are roped off, but overall the interaction with the wildlife is very intimate. There are a number of tours to Punta Tombo from both Puerto Madryn and Trelew, and they generally run between 120–160 pesos for a half-day tour. Some tours include the 35-peso park entrance fee and some do not, so be sure to do your research ahead of time.

Tea House in Gaiman

The only reason to visit Gaiman is to wander some lovely streets long enough to work up an appetite for cakes and jams and tortes and scones and more tea than you can handle. Teatime starts between 2:30 and 3 p.m., and for about 40–50 pesos you can fill yourself full of sweet things. For a more traditional experience, we recommend Gaiman's oldest teahouse, Plas y Coed (Yrigoyen 320, _www.plasycoed.com.ar_). The newest teahouse, Ty Cymraeg, boasts a traditional style with some modern twists, and the lemon pie is unreal!

Mathews 74, www.gaimantea.com
www.plasycoed.com.ar

Paleontological Museum

A small but fully stocked museum with loads of information about the region's rich past. There are more than 1,700 dinosaur fossils and 30 specimens of dinosaurs throughout the museum, and students and experts are often working on new projects as part of the exhibit. Admission is 35 pesos and the museum is open from 9 a.m. to 5 p.m.

Avenida Fontana 140
+54 (2965) 443-2100
www.mef.org.ar

ACCOMMODATION

El Agora

This cozy little hostel is the only one in Trelew. Basic but welcoming and friendly, this hostel offers all the necessities—Wi-Fi, stocked kitchen, lockers, tours, and breakfast with the added bonuses of bike tours and a flexible check-in and check-out schedule.

Cost: Dorms are 60 pesos and include breakfast.

From the bus terminal, walk three blocks north on Urquiza to Edwin Roberts. Take a left and you'll find the hostel three blocks down.

Edwin Roberts 33
+54 (0280) 442-6899
info@hostelagora.com
www.hostelagora.com

La Casona del Rio B&B

Located along the banks of the Chubut River, this beautiful house built in the beginning of the 20th century offers a home away from home. The couple who run the place, Norma and Carlos, are friendly and helpful, and Norma is reputedly an excellent cook. This is definitely not the traditional hostel feel, but if you're looking for nice, tranquil accommodation in Trelew, this is the place for you. Keep in mind that during the high season they do request a two-night minimum. If you intend to see Gaimin during your stay, this is also a great option as it is located between Trelew and Gaimin.

Cost: Slightly more than a hostel, this B&B is still the best deal in Trelew. Rates during the low season are 90 pesos for a single room, 110 pesos for a double and 135 pesos for a triple, and go up approximately 15 pesos a room in the high season. Rates include breakfast.

Approximately 5 km. outside of Trelew on Captain Murga Street (the main paved street leading to most of the tourist attractions), La Casona del Rio B&B is most easily accessed by taxi for 12 pesos.

Calle Capitán Murga 3998, Chacra 105
+54 (0280) 443-8348
hildyani@hotmail.com
www.lacasonadelrio.com.ar

CUYO

The Cuyo Province of Argentina is all about good wines and good times. The air is crisp, the people are friendly and there are plenty of opportunities to enjoy the beautiful outdoors. Whether you're traveling here to tour the famous vineyards of Mendoza, hike to the Andes, or slow down in a quiet town like La Rioja, this region of the country has more than enough to keep you entertained.

And shopping? Oh yeah. Save some room in your bag for the markets of Mendoza, where you're sure to find handcrafted, one-of-a-kind gifts to bring back to friends. With spectacular wine, cool summer nights and yummy street food, the Cuyo Province has a way of keeping you longer than you planned.

TOP ⭐ PICKS

Best Wine Tour by Bike:
Mr. Hugos in Mendoza

Best Street Food:
Super Pancho hotdogs

Best Way to Unwind:
Termas Cachueta in Mendoza

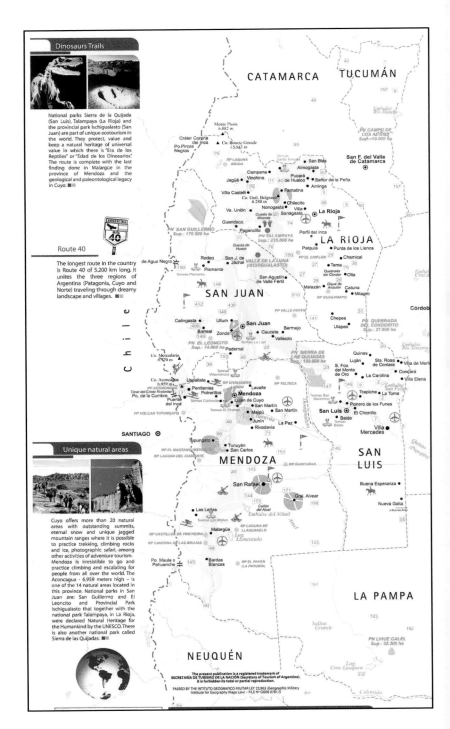

National parks Sierra de la Quijada (San Luis), Talampaya (La Rioja) and the provincial park Ischigualasto (San Juan) are part of unique ecotourism in the world. They protect, value and keep a natural heritage of universal value in which there is "Era de los Reptiles" or "Edad de los Dinosarios". The route is complete with the last finding done in Malargüe in the province of Mendoza and the geological and paleontological legacy in Cuyo.

Route 40

The longest route in the country is Route 40 of 5.200 km long. It unites the three regions of Argentina (Patagonia, Cuyo and Norte) traveling through dreamy landscape and villages.

Unique natural areas

Cuyo offers more than 20 natural areas with outstanding summits, eternal snow and unique jagged mountain ranges where it is possible to practice trekking, climbing rocks and ice, photographic safari, among other activities of adventure tourism. Mendoza is irresistible to go and practice climbing and escalating for people from all over the world. The Aconcagua - 6.959 meters high - is one of the 14 natural areas located in this province. National parks in San Juan are: San Guillermo and El Leoncito and Provincial Park Ischigualasto that together with the national park Talampaya, in La Rioja, were declared Natural Heritage for the Humankind by the UNESCO. There is also another national park called Sierra de las Quijadas.

MENDOZA

Mendoza is one of those cities that will give you a happy medium of everything: ample green spaces all over the city, swanky cafes and shops, wineries and adventures into the Andean peaks. Located right up against the Central Andes, it churns out roughly 70 percent of Argentina's phenomenal wine varietals. It is also home to Cerro Aconcagua, the Americas' tallest mountain peak. The city bustles, but not in a frantic pace like Buenos Aires, making it cosmopolitan and laidback enough to strike an interesting balance. Locals are stylish, deeply knowledgeable about food and wine, and as sweet as dulce de leche. The size of Mendoza helps it to maintain a cozy vibe, regardless of the weather. Spend your days according to your mood, since there is no shortage of activities to do. A leisurely walk along the tree-lined streets of downtown, market hopping, horseback riding, white water rafting, or wine tasting in the Uco Valley ... let your heart, or your inner sommelier, guide you!

HOW TO GET THERE

Mendoza is a fairly easy city to navigate, as it's not too big yet not too small. Mendoza has daily flights to Buenos Aires, and the Mendoza airport is 15 minutes outside of the city center by taxi and 30 minutes by public bus.

Bus
Take the 64 or 63 bus line to and from the airport for 1.40 pesos. The bus terminal is on the east end of town, within walking distance of the city center. Buses depart daily for Bariloche, Cordoba, and northern destinations daily.

City buses require either a bus card or pesos in the form of coins. If you do not have coins, get off the bus!

THINGS TO KNOW

- Because of its location right next to the Andes, Mendoza can get very cold in the fall/winter months of April-July. Pack accordingly.

- There are two main wine regions people visit: Maipu and the Uco Valley.

- Exercise caution in the larger parks during the day, as pickpocketing is on the rise.

- Mendoza has a large street dog population; do not be alarmed, as this is a widespread issue in this area of Argentina.

- Siesta reigns king here still, so if you need an item at a local store, go before 1 p.m. or after 6 p.m.

- You cannot leave Mendoza without doing are winery tour/ tasting and an extreme outdoor excursion into the nearby Andes. The area is famous for both!

THINGS TO DO

Parque General San Martin
This is one of the biggest parks in Latin America and it does not disappoint. This park houses Mendoza's futbol stadium and enumerable amounts of nooks and crannies to curl up on a bench for an afternoon nap. Visit the center of the park for a view of the lake or hire a bicycle and cruise to the top of the hill within the park itself. If you get hungry, flag down one of the vendors selling tasty street snacks. Watch your belongings while in this park.

Plaza Espana
Artistic murals, tiled patios and cute benches depicting the renewed fellowship between Spain and Argentina are all over this plaza. Located at Avenida Espana and Montevideo, is a good place to relax away the afternoon.

Secret Spot: For a nearby high-flying view of the city, head one block east to 948 Av. Espana. Duck into this fancy hotel, ride the elevator to the top floor into El Faro restaurant, and take in the panoramic view of Mendoza. Unless you want to pay for a pricy lunch, stop in between 11 a.m. and 2 p.m. for a little photo op.

Wine Tours
There are two main areas for wine tours; Maipu and the Uco Valley. Maipu has the bike tours, and a great set of vineyards with a few that are still family-owned. The Uco Valley sits higher

in the Andes, and thus has a whole other set of wine varietals to whet your whistle.

Wine Tours via Bike: Mr. Hugo's Wineries and Bikes

There are a host of "bikes and wine" tours you can do while in the famed vineyards of Mendoza. Senor Hugo is the man when it comes to wine tours. Hop on the 110 bus heading out of town and gently mention "Senor Hugo" to the driver. The bike rental shop is located in Mr. Hugo's and you will be pleasantly greeted with a complimentary glass of table wine. His family and friends can set up with a bike, helmet, water and a map of where the vineyards are.

Bike Rental: $9 USD/day.
Hours of Operation: Monday through Saturday 10 a.m.–6 p.m.
Entrance Fees: $5 USD/winery
Vineyard tour: $5–8 USD (30 minutes to one hour including a tasting)

2288 Urquiza
Maipu, Argentina
+54 (0261) 497-4067
www.mrhugobikes.com

Adventure in the Andes: Campo Base Travel and Adventure

They specialize in hostel-based package tours, such as trekking in the high Andes, rappelling, horseback riding, rafting, etc. The staff is super-helpful and extremely fun on the tours. They work closely with Hostelling International hostels, thus the staff is young and fun. Highly recommended!

466, Avenida Villanueva
Mendoza, Argentina
429-0775
info@campobase.com.ar
www.campobase.com.ar

Eat a Super Pancho!

While in Mendoza, spend 8 pesos and initiate yourself to these hot dogs, the Nathan's of Mendoza, on steroids. Request a "Super Pancho" and then step up to the plate to request which toppings you would like on your cheap, delectable treat. Toppings include chopped green olives, hot mayo, chimichurri, grilled onions, potato chips, and more. Best part about this situation? No closing time for afternoon siesta!

Take a "Mediacena"
All over Argentina, the mediacena, the pastry and coffee taken around 6 p.m., is customary to engage in for locals and travelers alike. Whether it is a coffee or a submarineo (steamed milk and chocolate bar), treat yourself right at one of Mendoza's romantic sidewalk cafes.

Go to the Hot Springs: Termas Cacheuta
This thermal spring is a 30-minute bus ride outside of town carved into the Andes. This manmade gem is a lovely way to pamper yourself after a hard day of trekking or an excursion of rappelling. There is a small fee to enter the park and it offers more than 10 pools of water at varying water temperature. Half of the pools are indoors; the other pools overlook the mountains. There is a restaurant at the springs as well as souvenir shops and an area to change.

Take a Fancy Cooking Course: Mendoza Wine Connection
Housed in the heart of the city inside of a gorgeous restored old home, they offer Argentinian cooking classes. The place is chic, with high ceilings, stained glass and funky modern art on the walls. If you are up for a new, creative way to spend your Friday night outside of the backpacker scene, then look no further than this cooking class. Chef Laura teaches the class three times per week and it runs from 5–9 p.m. She is just as charming as the food; you learn how to prepare dishes such as huemlo, empanadas and a proper bife de ojo in a small group setting. You are able to dive in and learn how to make every dish, while trying 4-5 different types of Malbec throughout the evening.

647 Sarmiento Street
Mendoza, Argentina
contact@mendozawineconnection.com

Gourmet Wine Tour: Ampora Wine Tours
If you're a wine aficionado or budding sommelier, go with this wine tour option over any bike wine tour. Ampora is located next door to the Mendoza Wine Connection. The staff is amazingly professional and will dazzle you with their wine knowledge. They have tour options into the Uco Valley or Maipu areas. Both options are of 5-star quality and include private bus transportation in small groups. These upscale tastings are accompanied by a gourmet

lunch and detailed explanation of what type of wine you are enjoying and how it was produced. Tours start at $160USD/day.

ACCOMMODATION

Mendoza Backpackers Hostel

Mendoza Backpacker's Hostel is part of the HI system. It is a nice combination of "party hostel" meets relaxed backpackers. They offer four to six person shared dorms with bathrooms en suite. You can opt for the female dorm room, but they do not have private room options. There is solid Wi-Fi connection, an activity every night to participate in with the partnering hostels, comfortable beds, glorious hot showers, and the ubiquitous ping-pong table. There is also a bar upstairs and rooftop seating for nice evenings.

Cost: 55–70 pesos for a shared dorm (low to high season); no private rooms offered.

San Lorenzo 19
Mendoza, Argentina
+54 (261) 429-4941
www.mendozabackpackers.com

International Mendoza Youth Hostel

This hostel is another great option for the HI cardholder, or someone who likes the standards to which HI requires of their hostels in terms of cleanliness and friendliness of staff. This hostel is brightly colored inside and a bit more raucous than others. Be prepared for a party and to stay up later because of dance parties or asados (BBQs) held inside the hostel. They have four-person dorm rooms with private bathrooms and double rooms as well. Breakfast is a good value and is included in your stay, along with free Wi-Fi, a pool, and 24-hour security and reception for coming home late at night. Take advantage of their tour packages.

Costs: 55 pesos for dorm rooms, 75 pesos for private rooms

Espana 343 Barrio Bombal, Mendoza
+54 (261) 424-0018
info@hostelmendoza.net

Bohemian Boutique Hotel

This 11-room intimate hotel is located in a quiet area of Mendoza very close to Parque General San Martin. Amir, the owner and his staff makes you feel at home as soon as you walk in the door, most likely because it actually was a home in the past. The rooms are designed using super-modern décor, chic artwork, and bright and fun colors. Here you will receive all the comforts of a normal swanky hotel stay: Wi-Fi, cable TV, pool, room service, big comfy bed, and a wonderfully cozy breakfast in the morning. It is also three blocks from the main street of restaurants and bars, Aristides Villanueva.

Cost: $95 USD for one night, but totally worth the splurge!

954 Granaderos
Mendoza 5500, Argentina
+54 (0261) 423-0575
www.bohemianboutiquehotel.
com

SHOPPING

Plaza Independencia
This outdoor market begins almost every night around 6 p.m. Live music fills the square almost every night around 8 p.m., and you can get a host of things ranging from a mate to souvenir bracelets to postcards, from handmade scarves to leather belts to artisan crafts. Snacks such as roasted peanuts, popcorn and *choripan* can be had for a few pesos.

Sarmiento Street
This is the main drag of town, tiled in cobblestone filtering into Plaza Independencia. Rightly so, as it is filled with swanky storefront windows that have the latest display of shoes, dresses, and leather items. Stop in for some great service and quality leather items and jewelry.

Cooking class in Mendoza

RESTAURANTS/BARS

Bonefide
A chain coffeehouse and chocolatier located all over Argentina, Bonefide is imperative for anyone looking to try her first or 10th *submarino*. They offer free Wi-Fi, warmth on those winter days, and some great promotions involving *medialunas* (croissants) and café con leche.

Chabuca
Chabuca is a Peruvian restaurant that has affordable, authentic cuisine. Opt for the ceviche and relive, or plan your trip to Peru while in Argentina!

96 Corrientes.

Govinda
In need of a purging from your last 10 Parrilla meals? Head over to this simple yet complex restaurant which boasts a variety of Indian and vegetarian dishes.

1777 Ave. San Martin, Godoy Cruz.

Irish Pub
Itching for a stellar stout or just a solid cocktail and some *papas fritas*? This Irish pub has a nice blend of locals and tourists alike on the restaurant street. They play American Top 40 hits along with the music video on the TVs. The atmosphere is chill and has a neighborhood feel. The Argentinian "Quilmes Rojo" is a solid drinking choice.

Located on Avenida Villanueva.

Bar Itaka
This bar has a slightly more upscale vibe and has the white linen to prove it. It features a cute outdoor seating section with umbrellas. Malbec is abundant and so is some language exchanges if you time it right! Couchsurfing hosts a weekly meetup of locals and travelers alike for a Spanish and English throwdown—one hour of Spanish, one hour of English. Check online for Couchsurfing's time frames.

On Avenida Villanueva.

LA RIOJA

La Rioja is one of the least populated provinces in Argentina, and even in the city, the streets are sparsely crowded and mellow. Sundays are especially quiet; during the slower tourist seasons, you can hear church sermons echoing out into the main plaza from the Basilica Menor de San Nicolas de Bari, a beautiful byzantine-style cathedral. The streets are lined with fragrant orange trees and you'll also find one of the most varied and high-quality fairs, or ferias, we've seen in this neck of the woods. The areas surrounding the city are home to wide spanning agricultural fields dedicated to green olives, cotton, and wine production. Stop in and check it out for a day, or three.

THINGS TO KNOW

- From February 17 to 20, La Rioja hosts Fiesta de la Chaya, complete with a music festival, parades and feasts.

- La Rioja is very arid and the heat in the summer months is intense. Make sure to pack appropriate clothes and sunscreen.

Dam los Sauces

This mountain-rimmed, man-made reservoir is considered an oasis in the summer, when La Rioja's unusually arid climate is at its hottest. The lake hosts an array of outdoor activities, including fishing, trekking, camping and windsurfing.

Museo de Arte Sacro

This sacred art museum contains five rooms showcasing religious art, altars, and ornate statues. Free to enter.

Located at Rivadavia 537.

························· **ACCOMMODATION** ·························

Apacheta Hostel

This family-owned hostel is one of the highlights of visiting La Rioja. It is thoughtfully designed in a modern spa-like motif, the dorm rooms are spacious, and the common rooms are small but inviting. There is a patio in the back, a fully stocked kitchen, and breakfast and Wi-Fi are included. It is located just a block away from the center, and the employees go above and beyond to help you navigate the town and the north of Argentina in general, with lots of great tips on where to go and what to see. It is a truly enjoyable stay.

Cost: 60–120 pesos

San Nicolas de Bari 669, La Rioja
+54 (038) 015-444-5445
www.facebook.com/apacheta-
hostel

SHOPPING

There is a pedestrian walkway located just off the main square on Buenos Aires Avda. with all of the pharmacies and clothing shops typical of the northern cities, but we recommend:

Feria del Productor al Consumidor

This fair had several phenomenal artisan meats and cheese booths that also offered a large selection of antipasti items, including olives, dried fruits, nuts and wine. There were also some great clothing items that were uncommon for the region and a smattering of typical gaucho gear, hand-woven scarves, and more. The days and hours seem to vary, so just take a stroll in that direction to see what's what.

Follow San Nicolas de Bari towards Av. 9 De Julio. Walk approximately three blocks, you will see another plaza come into view, and if the fair is running that day, it'll be hard to miss.

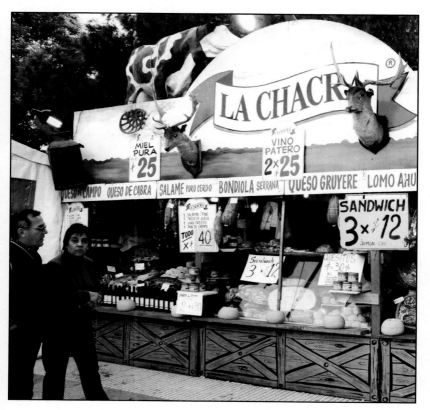

VOLUNTEERING IN ARGENTINA

Although Argentina is one of the more developed countries in South America, there are still areas, even within metropolitan Buenos Aires, that are socially marginalized and impoverished.

Volunteering is a wonderful way to break through cultural boundaries and get to know a culture from the inside-out.

We don't think that volunteering should cost you anything aside from basic costs to cover food and accommodation, and there are several local organizations in Argentina that share that belief.

From teaching English to helping care for howler monkeys, this list of nonprofits has a little bit of something for everyone. Contact these organizations yourself to see how you can help—you'll be glad you did.

TEACHING ENGLISH

B.A. English House
If you're interested in teaching English in Buenos Aires, B.A. English House offers classes for students age five and up. In exchange for your work, you'll be given Spanish immersion classes and the opportunity to take part in social activities.

Minimum Requirement: Six weeks, teaching at least 10 hours per week.
Cost: Varies
Based Out Of: Buenos Aires

englishhouse@ciudad.com.ar
www.baenglishhouse.com.ar

WORKING WITH CHILDREN

Union de los Pibes

This volunteer organization offers art, English, cooking and other classes as a way to provide a safe and fun environment for children.Volunteers are not required to have any language or teaching experience, just a willingness to be involved and help to give kids some stability. The club is currently working to fund a community center. Get in touch with them to see how you can help!

Minimum Requirement: 6 weeks
Cost: Free
Based Out Of: Buenos Aires

uniondelospibes@gmail.com
www.uniondelospibes.blogspot.com.ar

Conviven

Conviven is a nonprofit organization that works in youth development for residents of "Ciudad Oculta," a large shantytown that includes the poverty-stricken neighborhoods of Villa Lugano and Mataderos within Buenos Aires. Volunteers help with educational classes and cultural workshops like dance, music and arts education. Christian-influenced.

Minimum Requirement: None
Cost: Free
Based Out Of: Buenos Aires, near "Ciudad Oculta"

Martiniano Leguizamón 2974
CABA- Codigo Postal 1439
4686-5995
centro_conviven@yahoo.com.ar
www.conviven.org.ar

L.I.F.E. Argentina

This nonprofit works with children who live in areas of poverty, including Ciudad Oculta within Buenos Aires, providing education, recreation and social activities as well as food, clothing and supplies. They are 100 percent staffed by volunteers, and can almost always use a helping hand, whether teaching English, working in communications, or helping with social development.

Minimum Requirement: None
Cost: $25 USD 1–14 days; $50 USD 15 or more days.
Based Out Of: Buenos Aires

Pena 2121, Recoleta
4806-0640
futurevolunteers@lifeargentina.org
www.lifeargentina.org

COMMUNITY OUTREACH

Banco de Alimentos (Food Bank Foundation)

Most of the volunteer work with the Food Bank Foundation involves sorting and classifying donated food, checking for expiration dates, making community visits, working on resource development and helping the bank increase food distribution. No accommodation provided.

Minimum Requirement: None
Cost: Free
Based Out Of: Buenos Aires

Luis María Drago 5530, Villa Zagala, Partido de San Martín, C.P. 1650
Provincia de Buenos Aires
4724-2334 (calling from Buenos Aires)
rrhh@bancodealimentos.org.ar
www.bancodealimentos.org.ar

Red Solidaria (Solidarity Network)

This is a unique volunteer organization that connects people in need with those who can help. Designated call centers across the country dispatch information directing individuals to the appropriate agencies where they can find more information. Red Solidaria also works to mobilize social and community projects, including clothing drives and initiatives that help families affected by natural disasters.

Minimum Requirement: Varies
Cost: Free
Based Out Of: Buenos Aires, with work across the country

4761-7994
www.redsolidaria.org.ar

redsolidaria@fibertel.com.ar
www.redsolidaria.org.ar

Voluntario Global
This is a company that sets up local volunteer opportunities for low fees. Opportunities include working with orphan kids, teaching English, sustainable development, community work, journalism, marketing, HIV, health and prevention, and adult outreach. Program fees vary based on opportunity.

Minimum Requirement: Varies
Cost: $190 USD for four weeks, $270 USD for eight weeks, $390 USD for more than three months
Based Out Of: Buenos Aires

info@voluntarioglobal.com.ar
www.voluntarioglobal.org.ar

Academia Buenos Aires
Combine taking Spanish language courses with volunteering. Take a minimum of three weeks of Spanish classes, and Academia Buenos Aires will set you up with a free volunteer opportunity. Free to volunteer, but Spanish courses cost money. Accommodation may be provided for small fee.

Minimum Requirement: Three weeks
Cost: Free to volunteer, Spanish classes vary in cost
Based Out Of: Buenos Aires

Calle Hipólito Yrigoyen 571, piso 4
4345-5954
info@academiabuenosaires.com
www.academiabuenosaires.com

SET Idiomas—Learning Spanish
Study Spanish and volunteer in Córdoba in a variety of programs from social work to cultural development and non-formal education. Two weeks of Spanish courses required to be considered to volunteer. Volunteers must serve for one month.

Minimum Requirement: One month for volunteers; two weeks of Spanish to volunteer
Cost: Free to volunteer, cost for Spanish courses vary.
Based Out Of: Córdoba

Laprida 255
+ 54 (351) 469-1574
info@learningspanish.com.ar
www.learningspanish.com.ar

AGRICULTURE/ PERMACULTURE

Echo Village
If you're interested in permaculture, agriculture and living sustainability, volunteer your time at Echo Village. Free to volunteer, volunteers are asked to bring basic supplies such as toilet paper, sleeping bags, water, insect repellent, work boots. You can email ahead of time, or just show up to volunteer.

Minimum Requirement: One week
Cost: Free; May be fees for long-term volunteer stints and accommodation
Based Out Of: Tigre, Argentina

leonardojara27@hotmail.com
www.echo-village.blogspot.com

ANIMALS

Caraya Project—Volunteer with Black Howler Monkeys
Accommodation and food provided for minimum of three-week volunteer program. Shared room with rustic accommodation. Work includes preparing food, cleaning and caring for monkeys and other animals living on farm (lion, llamas, pumas, ducks, chickens).

Minimum Requirement: Three weeks
Cost: $625 USD for three weeks, $750 for one month and $1125 for three months
Based Out Of: La Cumbre, Córdoba

carayaproject@yahoo.com.ar
www.volunteer-with-howler-monkeys.org

FOOD & RECIPES

When you tell most people that you are going to Argentina as a vegetarian, the usual response is a chuckle, followed by "good luck!" The truth is, it is pretty easy to stay veggie while you travel. Here are some tips to help you.

EATING IN

- Cooking for yourself is the easiest and cheapest way to get fed while you travel.

- Fruit and veggie stands are everywhere, in just about every city, and the bonus here is that they are cheap. You can buy all the trimmings for a great salad for less than three dollars.

- Grocery stores also carry everything necessary to make healthy vegetarian meals, and you can even find vegetarian *milanesa* in many stores. Things like tofu and legumes are less common, but you can still find plenty of other sources of protein.

- Health stores are common in the larger cities and have multiple soy-based treats, including veggie burgers. They also have iron supplements and vitamins.

- Ferias (artisanal fairs) are amazing in Argentina, and have heaps of herbs, spices, produce, pickled veggies and cheeses. In the north you can find Andean potatoes that come in a rainbow of colors, and they are seriously delicious.

This is where you have to use your noggin a little more. While it is still a budding trend in Argentina, it is becoming more and more common for restaurants to offer great vegetarian options. Parrillas are the most difficult restaurants to find a good veggie meal, but it's still possible to eat.

• Menus are, obviously, written in Spanish and it can be tough to crack the code to know whether or not you are ordering correctly. Simply letting the waiter know "*soy vegetariana*" or "*quiero algo sin carne*" is the best way to handle it.

• There are nearly always vegetarian empanadas and quiche-like pastries, but they are pretty rich and the body needs greens!

• Many of the restaurants in Argentina are influenced by Italian cuisine, where there are several meatless options. In northern Argentina we found the most satisfying options for vegetarians: quinoa burgers, awesome squash dishes and some of the best potatoes ever.

• Salads in most restaurants are lacking—usually they consist of iceberg lettuce, white onion and tomato slices—but you can usually jazz it up a bit if you know how to ask. Here is a list of common vegetarian menu items.

Carrots – *zanahoria*
Egg – *huevo*
Squash – *calabaza*
Beets – *remolacha*
Olives – *aceitunas*
Potatoes – *papas or patates*
Onion – *cebolla*
Bell peppers – *pimientos*
Avocado – *palta*
Basil – *albahaca*
Roasted vegetables – *verduras de horno*
Grilled vegetables – *verduras a la parrilla*

Steak, steak and more steak. They love their meat in Argentina. Check out our "Carne 101" for tips on what and how to order. Aside from the beef, what's there to eat?

Empanadas
Empanadas are pastries usually filled with beans, yellow corn, beef, chorizo, bacon, or pumpkin. There are thousands of variations on the empanada, so ask ahead before you purchase to make sure it's what you want. They can be either sweet or savory.

Medialunas
Sweet croissants that are common staples for breakfast. Breakfasts are usually very light and include tea and coffee and a medialuna.

Asado (Barbecue) Items
Asados are very common throughout Argentina. They're basically big cookouts where the meat is slow-roasted while participants drink beer and get dinner ready. It's a tradition that takes hours, and menu items usually include steak, sausages, *mollejas* (thymus glands), pork, and chicken. If you can't make it to a local asado, you can order asado menu items from restaurants known as *parrillas*.

Milanesa
This is a process for cooking just about any kind of meat that involves dipping the cut of meat into egg and salt and then lightly breading and frying it. If you want to get really gourmet, order *Milanesa Nepolitana* and you'll get ham, cheese, and tomato on top!

Tartas
Tartas are basically quiches with less egg and more fillings. Tartas can include a variety of ingredients, including tomato, ham, basil, mushroom, pumpkin, squash or zucchini.

Pizza
It's surprising, a bit, but the pizza in Argentina is actually really tasty, provided you keep this in mind: pizzas usually have a thicker crust and they're usually lacking in red sauce. Sometimes you'll find pizza restaurants with interesting toppings, such as green olives

(pitted, even). Ask a local for recommendations on their favorite pizza joint, as they range in quality and price.

Locro
You'll most frequently find this thick stew in the northern provinces of Argentina. It's generally filled with rice, vegetables and corn. Yum!

Dulce de Leche
This sweet liquid caramel-like dessert is found throughout all of Argentina and it's delicious. You can use it as a spread for bread or crackers, or enjoy it in some of Argentina's other desserts.

Alfajor
Alfajors, popular Argentine cookies, almost always have a dulce de leche spread.

Ice Cream
You'll find some of the world's best ice cream and gelato throughout Argentina, specifically in Patagonia, where ice cream and chocolate shops are a dime a dozen. Sweet tooth? Be sure to visit San Carlos de Bariloche.

ARGENTINE CARNE 101:

Argentines love their meat—all of it. Most Argentines think a meal without meat is not worth the time, and both home and restaurant menus reflect their passion for the stuff. Here are a couple tips to help you navigate the many, many choices for both types and methods of preparing meat.

Bondiolas
Usually served as a sandwich, this is tender cut of pork shoulder cooked slowly on the grill. When you order it, they cut a chunk and crisp it before tossing it onto some French bread and letting you spice it up with condiments of your choice.

Asados
Perhaps the most popular method for preparing meat in A rgentina, this basically refers to the process of slow-grilling a huge chunk (sometimes the whole animal) of any kind of meat. More traditional asados use native trees as they emit a strong-smelling smoke and further flavor the meat. Spiced primarily with salt, the meat comes out tender and packed full of its natural flavor.

Colita de Cuadril
This is the tail end of the rump, also known as tri-tip. It's tender, juicy and usually pretty lean compared to some of the other cuts.

Bife de Chorizo
Lots of people pass this up because they think chorizo is sausage. In Argentina, however, bife de chorizo refers to the sirloin strip (similar to a N.Y. strip), a tender and delicious cut of meat, also slowly cooked on the grill and lightly seasoned.

Bife de Lomo
A very lean cut of meat and usually one of the most tasty. However, it's also one of the most expensive.

ORDER IT:

jugoso – rare • *a punto* – medium rare • *bien cocido* – well done

LOCAL RECIPES

Some of these classic Argentine dishes are a little time-consuming, but well worth the wait. Invite over friends and make a night of it. Include some Malbec wine to emulate a true Argentine meal.

Empanadas hot from the oven.

Classic Meat Empanadas

Makes 20 empanadas

1 package Goya tapas de
   empañadas (premade
   empanada shells)
1 lb. ground beef
1 large white onion diced
2 scallions diced
2 cloves garlic minced
½ red bell pepper diced

½ green bell pepper diced
2 tbs. safflower oil
1 ½ tsp. black pepper
1 ½ tsp. paprika
1 tsp. salt
½ tsp. ground cumin
½ cup tomato purée

optional: ½ cup raisins, green olives cut into pieces, 3 hardboiled eggs diced.

Sauté the onions, shallots and garlic in a sauté pan with safflower oil until fragrant. Add bell peppers and sauté until all vegetables are tender and onion is translucent. Add tomato purée. Add ground beef and cook until browned. Mix in salt and spices.

Let filling cool to room temperature and mix in raisins, olives and egg. Preheat oven to 350F.

Lay empanada shell in hand and spoon filling into center. Bring edges together (creating a half-moon shape) and pinch along the edge, creating a seal. Start at one side of the seal and fold dough over in small turns repeatedly (creating the spiral look shown in picture), or press edges with a fork for a more simple finish.

Place empanadas on a floured cookie sheet and brush tops with a beaten egg. Bake at 300 degrees for 15 to 20 minutes.

replace meat with well drained (press the moisture out) creamed corn mixed with grated fresh corn for a traditional vegetarian option.

In Argentina you can tell what kind of base filling is in empanadas by the way it is closed.

Spiral closing on side = beef
Spiral closing facing up = chicken
Closed with fork crimping = pork
Spiral closing/round or horn shape = vegetable or cheese

Lentil Stew

Serves 6

¼ lb. lentils
1 med. onion diced
1 red bell pepper diced
1 green bell pepper diced
1 carrot cut in slices
2 cups peeled and diced squash
2 garlic cloves minced
½ cup tomato purée
1 chorizo (sausage) cubed
3 ½ oz. bacon cubed
1 bouillon cube
salt, pepper, and cumin to taste

Soak lentils in cold water overnight. Drain and rinse. Place lentils in large stockpot and cover with fresh water. Cook over medium low heat for 20 minutes (without salt).

Meanwhile, heat just enough oil to cover bottom of a sauté pan and add onion, peppers and garlic. Cook until onions are translucent. Add to lentils, then add the rest of the ingredients.

In another pan, heat the sausage and bacon until they release their fat and get a little crispy. Drain excess fat and add them to the pot.

Cover with water and simmer for 1 to 1 ½ hours, stirring occasionally. Stew should have a good amount of liquid. If cooked down, add water as needed.

Simply leave out meat and use vegetable bouillon to make vegetarian stew.

Alfajores de Dulce de Leche
(Cookies with caramel)

Makes 40 alfajores

Chimichurri Sauce

1 tsp. oregano
1 tsp. paprika
1 tsp. crushed red pepper flakes
1 small bunch of flat leaf parsley – leaves only
3 garlic cloves
¼ red onion
salt and pepper to taste
3 tbs. white wine vinegar
1 cup corn oil

Soak the oregano, parsley and red pepper flakes in lukewarm water for 10 minutes. Mix well and drain. Add the rest of the ingredients.

Let steep for 12 hours and transfer to a bottle for storage.

*All recipes provided by Norma Soued. For fun and informative cooking classes in Argentina, visit www.argentinecookingclassses2.com. *

Spinach and Ricotta Tart

Serves 4

3 tbs. butter
1 cup white onion diced
2 garlic cloves minced
1 tsp. salt
½ tsp. nutmeg
2 10-ounce pkgs. Frozen spinach or chard, thawed and drained
1 cup ricotta cheese
½ cup grated Parmesan cheese
6 eggs
Egg wash: 1 egg beaten
2 round sheets of puff pastry

Sauté onion and garlic in butter until soft and slightly golden. Add salt and nutmeg. Add spinach and cook for one minute. Remove from heat and let cool. Mix ricotta, Parmesan and 2 eggs in large bowl. Add cooled spinach to the cheeses and season with salt and pepper to taste.

Preheat oven to 400F.

Roll out one of the pastry sheets into a circle about 14 inches in diameter. Drape pastry over a 9-inch tart pan with a removable bottom, pressing pastry into bottom and sides of pan. Fill tart with spinach/cheese mixture.

Place 4 eggs (unbeaten) equally on top of the mixture. Sprinkle with Parmesan.

Roll out other piece of puff pastry into a 9-inch circle and place on top of tart. Create a seal by crimping the edges together.

Brush top with egg wash and use a fork to prick a few holes in the top of the tart as vents.

Lower oven temperature to 350F and bake for 40 minutes. Cool in pan for 30 minutes before lifting the tart out of the tart pan.

Q&A
MEET A LOCAL

LUCHI GONZALEZ CARO, MEDICA

Luchi Gonzalez Caro is a local Argentine from Mashwitz, 90 km. north of Buenos Aires, who works in the medical industry. Read on to learn more about medical care, including abortion, and what she thinks are the best and worst things about Buenos Aires.

GGG: What do you do in Buenos Aires?

I do medical work for a company in Buenos Aires, examining around 30 patients each day for general health concerns/issues. I recently finished my studies, but next year will return for my specialization—probably in infections medicine.

GGG: What are the things you love and hate about Buenos Aires?

I love the access to cultural events like concerts, theater, libraries—there is a lot to do in Buenos Aires. I like that at any

hour that you want to go to a bar or a coffee shop, there is somewhere open where you can have a drink and chat with friends.

I don't like that there are so many people, that the city is dirty and that public transportation is awful during rush hour.

GGG: When you are traveling, what do you miss most about Argentina?

Mate. Not just the tea, but the pastime and what it means. I didn't just miss the tea, but the chance to sit around and chat with friends. When we were in Mexico, we brought along mate and when we would have it out, other people from Argentina would flock to join us. It's about the tradition and the event more than the tea.

GGG: When people are traveling to Argentina, what recommendations do you have for the ways they can best blend in and show respect to locals?

I think the biggest thing is just to remember that you are in another country and although people may not remember you, you do make an impression. I think it is common for travelers, especially in large groups, to forget about the people around them and get very loud or rude sometimes. Especially on public transit, you'll blend in most and show the most respect if you keep your voice down a bit and don't demand a lot of attention.

GGG: Can you talk a bit about the health system in Argentina (Buenos Aires)?

Health care is free in Argentina, and I think this is really important. However, there is also private health care, and for the most part the only people who use public health care are from the lower class. In Argentina, it is commonly known that the level of service provided in public health facilities is at least as good as that of

private centers. The biggest problem is access to materials; the government has a very small budget for health care and so the public hospitals often run out of space and supplies. Additionally, not enough emphasis is put on prevention, and things like birth control and sex education, especially for people with less money and education. When I was working at the hospital during my studies, we didn't see many people from the middle class, and a lot of that has to do with their access to prevention education.

GGG: Does this mean someone traveling to Argentina, an extranjera, can receive free medical care?

Yes. If you go into the hospital with an emergency you will be taken care of, whether you can pay or not. A lot of people from Paraguay, Uruguay and Bolivia come here for exactly that reason.

GGG: In terms of women's health, how accessible is birth control?

In theory, everyone has access to free birth control, but many people, especially in the lower class, aren't aware. Additionally, when you work in Argentina you pay into a health insurance plan that also grants you access to birth control.

GGG: Abortions are illegal in Argentina. Are they happening anyway?

Yes, of course. They are illegal (except in very rare circumstances), but they're happening and everyone knows they happen. The thing is, you receive the kind of abortion you can pay for. So, people in the lower class run a huge risk of very dangerous abortions performed by unqualified doctors or performed at home through various word-of-mouth methods. People with a lot of money can pay for a more traditional/safe abortion, but they're still prohibited.

Q&A
MEET AN EXPAT

KRISTIN GUTEKUNST, 28
New York City

Kristin Gutekunst moved to Buenos Aires last year and has quickly made her mark on the Buenos Aires social scene. She's had so much success here that she's launched two businesses, GlowMeBaires and NailMeBaires. Here, she gives us the low-down on how to orient yourself to Buenos Aires, and what to know about sexy Argentine lovers.

GGG: When and how did you land in Buenos Aires, and what were your first impressions?

I arrived in Buenos Aires in September 2011 to start a master's program with UNSAM and Georgetown University in Development Management and Policy. I was lucky enough to have friends here who helped me orient and integrate immediately. They were Argentine, American, and from other Latin American countries. Through these contacts I got a job teaching English on Skype and my roommate became a tour guide with a tourist company, Biking Buenos Aires.

GGG: Describe life in BsAs? Do you feel like you "mesh"? What do you do with your time, how do you get around, how do you make the big bucks, etc.?

The first few essentials to becoming integrated in Buenos Aires are buying a cell phone (the cheapest and most reliable model costs about 200 pesos); and buying a GuiaT (the "bible" of getting around by colectivo or subway). Many people also don't know about www.mapa.buenosaires.gov.ar/—a great Internet website which will tell you how to get around. And if you plan to be here longer, the city has a pretty impressive bike lane system—a great way to navigate around the rush hour traffic. Wear a helmet, though; drivers are very aggressive here and the pedestrian doesn't really have the right of way.

Buenos Aires has a huge ex-pat community that is extremely supportive and helpful to newcomers and immediately adopts those as their own. It's a great way to find community as soon as you arrive. I suggest checking out Vitruvian—a cross-fit boot camp in Palermo and Puerto Madero; The Buenos Aires Pub Crawl; and Buenos Aires Futbol Amigos to name a few. The city also runs on Facebook events, groups and fan pages to get the word out, so be sure to like all the pages of your favorite clubs, restaurants or other groups to be "in the know."

As should be clear by now, there is a lot of opportunity in Buenos Aires. It is the perfect place to try something new, to learn a new language, dance, instrument, or craft. Many of my friends are artistically oriented and have formed bands, have their own private photography companies or sell hot sauce in San Telmo. I personally am in the midst of launching NailMeBaires, a designer nail painting business; and GlowMeBaires, a fluorescent accessory business (currently including black light reflective sunglasses, face painting, and hoping to expand into other areas). Like I said, opportunities are endless here!

GGG: Have you visited an OBGYN? What was the experience like? What about other girl stuff?

I haven't visited an OBGYN in BsAs yet. I arrived with a prescription for my birth control in the U.S. I tried to have it filled in multiple pharmacies but was told that I needed to find the exact chemical makeup so they could find a generic version. After doing so, I was told they didn't have any drug resembling mine and that I would have to visit an OBGYN to have a new prescription written. I gave up and opted to use condoms as a way to stay safe. Luckily, the men I have dated here are good about using condoms. They almost always have them stashed away somewhere and are not shy about going to buy them if they don't.

GGG: Do you think dating here is any different than dating back home?

I recently became single and have just started dating Argentine men. My experience thus far, and that of many friends I have compared notes with, is that if they have traveled or had experience with foreign women, they are usually very fair and respectful in bed.

Those who have not, and especially men from Buenos Aires, tend to lean toward one night stands, less personal sex, and sex which is really one-sided in terms of pleasure. There is also no such thing as platonic friendships with the opposite sex: a man either wants to be friends with you because he wants to sleep with you, or he is gay. Like I said, I am relatively new on the dating scene, so still waiting for one to prove me wrong!

Also, I should mention that BsAs is an extremely gay-friendly city. There is lots of nightlife oriented towards the LGBT scene, and people are very accepting. It is my impression that many other Latin Americans flock towards the city to study, work and many eventually stay, as other countries are not as friendly.

GGG: What's your biggest piece of advice for female travelers/ expats in BA?

The minute you get here, take a tour or join in a class or club—you will find friends immediately and they will help you get adjusted, even if it's for one night.

LANGUAGE

.... **PRONUNCIATION** ....

Having some Spanish under your belt for travel in Argentina is highly recommended, if not essential. You *can* get around with English, but you'll miss out on so many opportunities. You don't have to master the language, but take some courses to at least have a strong hold of the basics. It's worth it!

You've probably also heard by now that Argentine Spanish is very distinct. Referred to as Castellano, the pronunciation is unique, primarily in that "ll," usually pronounced "ya," is pronounced "ch," while "y", usually pronounced the same as in English, is generally pronounced with more of a "ge" sound.

Otherwise, Spanish is pretty straightforward when it comes to pronunciation. Words are pronounced exactly how they are spelled, and there are very few, if any, exceptions. Start by memorizing vowel sounds:

A = ahh

E = ehh

I = eee

O = oh

U = ooo

Airport: *Aeropuerto*

Bus Station: *Terminal de Omnibus*

Boat: *Barco*

Ferry: *El transbordador*

Hello: *Hola*

Goodbye: *Chau*

See you later: *Nos vemos*

Yes: *Si*

No: *No*

Please: *Por favor*

Thank you: *Gracias*

Thank you very much: *Muchas gracias*

Excuse me: *Perdon, Disculpa*

Excuse me (as in, can you repeat that?): *Como?*

Where is...?: *Donde esta...?*

How much...?: *Cuanto cuesta?*

How can I get there?: *Como puedo llegar?*

I'm sorry: *Lo siento, or perdon*

Why?: *Porque?*

Where is the bathroom?: *Donde esta el bano?*

Left: *Izquierda*

Right: *Derecha*

Straight: *Derecho*

I need help: *Necessito ayuda*

Let's Go: *Vamos*

Ashtray: *Sinisero*

Tip: *Propina*

Morning-After Pill: *Pastilla de dia despues:*

Condom: *Forro/preservativo*

SHOPPING

How much is this?: *Cuanto cuesto? Or Cuanto sale?*

It's too expensive: *El es muy caro.*

Can you discount this?: *Puede ser menos? Hay discuento?*

Can you help me please?: *Me puede ayudar por favor?*

I'm just looking: *Solo estoy mirando*

Do you have something bigger/smaller?: *Tienes algo mas grande/chico?*

I'll come back: *Vuelvo/regreso/voy a dar la vuelta*

I like this: *Me gusta*

It's very beautiful: *Es muy bonita*

NUMBERS

0: zero	**14:** catorce	**100:** cien
1: uno	**15:** quince	**200:** doscientos
2: dos	**16:** diez y seis	**300:** trescientos
3: tres	**17:** diez y siete	**400:** cuatrocientos
4: cuatro	**18:** diez y ocho	**500:** quinientos
5: cinco	**19:** diez y nueve	**600:** seiscientos
6: seis	**20:** veinte	**700:** setecientos
7: siete	**30:** treinta	**800:** ochocientos
8: ocho	**40:** cuarenta	**900:** novecientos
9: nueve	**50:** cincuenta	**1,000:** mil
10: diez	**60:** sesenta	**2,000:** dos mil
11: once	**70:** setenta	**3,000:** tres mil
12: doce	**80:** ochenta	**4,000:** cuatro mil
13: trece	**90:** noventa	**5,000:** cinco mil

...And so on

GENERAL RULE FOR NUMBERS BELOW 100:

21: twenty + 1 = *veinte y uno*

46: forty + 6 = *cuarenta y seis*

79: seventy + 9 = *setenta y nueve*

GENERAL RULE FOR NUMBER ABOVE 100:

120: one hundred + 20 = *ciento veinte*

260: two hundred + 60 = *doscientos sesenta*

480: four hundred + 80 = *cuatrocientos ochenta*

RESTAURANTS

Can I have more?: *Puedo tener mas?*

Is it spicy?: *Se pica?*

Plate: *plato*

It's delicious: *Es muy rico*

May I have a menu?: *Puedo ver la carta?*

I don't eat meat: *No como carne*

I am a vegetarian: *Soy vegetariana*

Can I pay with a credit card?: *Puedo pagar con tarjeta de credito?/Aceptan tarjetas de credito?*

The check, please: *La cuenta, por favor*

With/Add: *Con*

Without: *Sin*

FEELINGS

I like: *Me gusta*

I don't like: *No me gusta*

This is fun: *Es divertido*

I'm hungry: *Tengo hambre*

I'm hot: *Tengo calor/hace calor*

I'm cold: *Tengo frio/hace frio*

I want to go: *Quiero ir*

I'm sick: *Estoy enferma/me siento enferma*

My head hurts: *Duele mi cabeza*

I love Argentina: *Me encanta Argentina*

I miss...: *Extrano... (Te extrano: I miss you)*

SLANG (*JERGA*)

We can't fit it all here, of course, but this should get you started.

For some more great Argentine slang, check out: *www.argentineslang.wordpress.com*

If you're really interested in local jargon, there's a book available on Amazon called "Che Boludo: A Gringo's Guide to Understanding Argentines" by James Bracken.

Buenos: *Good morning, day, night*

Que tal?: *How's it going?*

Como andas?: *How are you?*

Suerte: *Bye (literally, "good luck")*

Que haces: *What are you up to?*

Che boludo/a: *Informal greeting used among friends (direct translation: what's up big balls?)*

Flaco/flaca: *Another, slightly less offensive, informal greeting (direct translation: thin boy/girl)*

Pedo: *Used for a number of occasions, primarily to refer to being drunk (en pedo) or not even drunk (ni en pedo), or when* someone's not doing anything or is a bit useless (al pedo).

Pucho: *cigarette*

If you're looking for all the naughty words, we highly recommend just attending a fútbol match and taking notes. *"Hijo de mil putas"* should get you started…

A

Abortion, 25–26, 34–35, 249
Academia Buenos Aires, 227
Accommodations, 10, 38, 40. *See also under specific location or region, e.g.: Buenos Aires*
Advice Book Shop (Santa Fe), 111
Agriculture volunteer programs, 228
Air travel, 47, 78, 191, 196, 202
Alcohol, 12, 205
beer, 51, 100, 111
wine, 37, 142, 183, 209, 213–215
Alfajores de Dulce de Leche (recipe), 243
Alfonsín, Raúl, 59
Alligators, 123
Almerco (El Bolson), 188
Alpaca goods, 164
Alta Córdoba, 98
Alto-Rosario, 109
Amphitheater, 143
Ampora Wine Tours, 215–216
Andes Mountains, 147, 148, 160, 212
Animal welfare volunteer programs, 228
Antique market (San Telmo), 89

Antiques, 38, 82, 89, 121
Apartment rental, 40–41
Archaeological museums, 151, 166
Architecture, 119
Argentina
history of, 58–59
provinces and capitals, 48
Art galleries and museums, 80, 81, 111, 220
Arte Buenos Aires, 50
Artist community (El Bolson), 185
Arts fair (El Bolson), 188
ATMs, 38
Avenida Argentina (Neuquén), 182
Avenida Cabildo (Belgrano), 86

B

B.A. English House (Buenos Aires), 223
Bakeries, 199
Balcony of the Valley (Neuquén), 182
Banco de Alimentos (Buenos Aires), 226
Banco de las Animales, 116
Bancos del Carbillo, 116
Bar Itaka

(Mendoza), 218
Bariloche. see San Carlos de Bariloche
Barrancas de Belgrano, 85
Barrio la Perla (Mar de Plata), 119
Bars, 19, 218
Basilica Menor de San Nicholas de Bari (La Rioja), 219
Beaches, 107, 116, 119, 130–131
Beagle Channel, 203
Bed bugs, 28–29
Beer, 51, 100, 111
Belgrano (Buenos Aires), 23, 85–86
Belongings, protecting your, 18–19
"Best of" awards, 37–38
Bicycle rental, 110, 143, 179, 214
Bicycle tours, 80, 143, 209, 213–214
Birth control, 26, 35, 249, 251–252
Blogs, 44, 53
Boat tours
Beagle Channel, 203
Iguazu Falls, 126
River Paraná, 107–108, 111, 113
Boca Juniors, 63
Bodega Nanni (Cafayate), 143

Bolivia, 49
Bonefide
    (Mendoza), 218
Books, 52, 111
Border crossings,
    49–50, 132
Borges y Alvarez
    Libro Bar (El
    Calafate), 199
Bosques de
    Palermo, 82
Botanical garden
    (Tilcara), 162
Boulevard Galvez
    (Santa Fe), 111
Bracken, James,
    52
Brazil, 125
Breweries, 111
Budget travel, 42
Buenos Aires,
    73–95, 247–248,
    250–251
accommodations,
    83–84, 86, 88–89,
    91–92, 94–95
activities, 82,
    85–87, 90, 93
attractions, 80–81
Belgrano, 85–86
cosmetic tourism,
    30–33
El Centro/Retiro,
    92–95
layout, 74
Palermo, 82–84
Recoleta, 90–92
safety and secu-
    rity, 74–75
San Telmo, 87–89
shopping, 38, 84,
    86, 89, 92, 95
top picks, 74
tours, 80

transportation,
    78–79
volunteer pro-
    grams, 223,
    225–227
Buenos Aires Gay
    Pride Festival, 51
Buenos Aires World
    Tango Festival,
    50
Buses, 47
Buenos Aires, 78,
    80
Cuyo, 212
Entre Rios, 106,
    110, 113, 115,
    119
Jujuy province,
    161
Litoral, 125, 126
Patagonia, 176–
    177, 182, 185,
    191, 194, 196,
    202, 205
safety on, 15–17
Salta province,
    138, 147, 150

C
Cabo Vírgenes,
    200–201
Cachi, 138,
    145–146
Cafayate, 37, 138,
    142–144
Camera repair, 45
Campo Base
    Travel and
    Adventure
    (Mendoza), 214
Capybara, 108
Car rental, 175
Caraya Project
    (Córdoba), 228

Carino, Giselle,
    30–31
Carne, 236
Carnival de Pais
    (Gualeguay-
    chu), 50
Carnival Festival,
    50, 98, 129, 161
Cascada de los
    Duendes (San
    Carlos de Bari-
    loche), 179
Cascada Escon-
    dida, 100
Castellano, 255
Catamarca,
    149–151
Catcalls, 13–15,
    68, 168
Catedral Basillica
    (Salta), 139
CDC (Center for
    Disease Control),
    10
Cell phones, 42,
    251
Cementerio El
    Salvador (San
    Salvador de
    Jujuy), 157
Cemeteries, 90,
    157
Center for Disease
    Control (CDC),
    10
Cerrado Campa-
    nario, 178
Cerro de Los Siete
    Colores, 153, 159
Cervecería Santa
    Fe, 111
Chatwin, Bruce, 52
Che Boludo
    (James

Bracken), 52
Chicoanas, 145
Children, volun-
    teer programs
    with, 225–226
Chile, 177
Chinatown (Bel-
    grano), 85
Chocolate, shop-
    ping for, 181
Churches
Buenos Aires, 86,
    93
Jujuy province,
    159
Salta province,
    139, 146, 151
"Ciudad Oculta"
    (Buenos Aires),
    225
Classic Meat
    Empanadas
    (recipe), 239
Clerica, 107
Climate, 45, 219
Cold-weather
    gear, 205
Colectivos, 78
Colón, 115–118
Colonia Suiza
    (San Carlos
    de Bariloche),
    178–179, 181
Communication,
    safety and, 13
Community
    outreach volun-
    teer programs,
    226–228
Condoms, 26,
    252
Consulates, 10,
    20

Contraception,
    26, 35, 249,
    251–252
Conviven
    (Buenos Aires),
    225
Cooking classes,
    215
Córdoba, 38,
    97–103
accommoda-
    tions, 101–102
activities, 99–100
shopping,
    102–103
top picks, 97
travel tips, 98
volunteer pro-
    grams, 227–228
Corrientes,
    129–131
Cosmetic
    tourism, 32–35
Cosmetics, 47
Couchsurfing,
    9–10
Country code, 42
Craft fairs. See
    also Handcraft
    markets
Jujuy province,
    37, 160, 164,
    167
Patagonia, 181,
    184, 188
Culture, 57–70
catcalls, 68
and customs, 57
The Dirty War, 60
drugs, 69
Falkland Island
    conflict, 62
family and reli-

gion, 57
gauchos, 64
greetings, 57–58
history of Argen-
    tina, 58–59
mate, 65–67
of police, 68–69
and politics,
    61–62
sensitive topics,
    63
sex and sexuality,
    68
Currency ex-
    change, 38–39
Customs, 57
Cuyo, 209–221
accommoda-
    tions, 216–217,
    220
activities, 213–
    216, 220
La Rioja, 219–221
Mendoza,
    212–218
restaurants and
    bars, 218
shopping, 217,
    221
top picks, 209
transportation,
    212
travel tips, 212–
    213, 219

D
Dam los Sauces
    (La Rioja), 220
Dance classes,
    44
Dating, 252
Day of Remem-
    brance for Truth

and Justice, 60
Day trips
Córdoba, 97,
99–100
Corrientes,
130–131
El Bolson, 186
Rio Gallegos,
200–201
Tucuman, 169
Dengue fever, 24
Desaparecedos,
60
The Devil's Throat
(Tilcara), 162
Dining, 218. See
also Food
Directions, asking
for, 14
The Dirty War, 59,
60
Dress, appropri-
ate, 13, 20
Driving, 175
Drugs, 12, 69

E
Echo Village
(Tigre), 228
Eco-tours, 115
El Anfiteatro (Ca-
fayate), 143
El Bolson, 37, 174,
185–188
El Bosque Tallado
(El Bolson),
186–187
El Calafate,
196–199
El Centro (Buenos
Aires), 74, 92–95
El Cerro San
Javier, 169
El Chalten, 38,

193–195
El Hielo Azul (El
Bolson), 187
El Lago del Desi-
erto, 194
El Museo Pa-
leontológico Mu-
nicipal Ernesto
Bachman
(Neuquén),
182–183
El Nevado, 145
El Obelisco de
Buenos Aires (El
Centro), 93
El Parque Nacio-
nal del Tierra del
Fuego (Ushuaia),
203
El Parque Nacio-
nal Los Alceres,
189, 192
El Plaza Central
(Tilcara), 164
El Practico, 126
El Refugio Piltriq-
uitron (El Bolson),
186
El Secreto de Sus
Ojos (film), 52
Electrical voltage,
45
Electronics, 205
Embassies, 10, 20,
82
Emergency ser-
vices, 11
English language,
teaching, 223
Entre Rios, 105–121
accomodations,
108–109, 112,
114, 117, 120–121
activities, 107–108,

111, 113–114,
116, 119
Colón, 115–118
Mar de Plata,
118–121
Paraná, 113–115
Rosario, 105–109
Santa Fe, 110–112
shopping, 109,
112, 115, 118,
121
top picks, 106
transportation,
106, 110, 113,
115, 119
travel tips, 106,
110, 115, 119
Espina, Veronica
Obrador, 54–55
Esquel, 191–193
Esteros de Iberá
Wetlands (Mer-
cedes), 123, 130
Eva Perón
Museum
(Palermo), 51
Evita (Eva Perón),
51, 58, 90
Evita (film), 52
Expatriate (expat),
Q&A with,
250–252

F
Falkland Islands,
62, 63
Family, 57
Fashion, 54–55, 84
Feitlowit, Margue-
rite, 52
Feminine hygiene
products, 27, 178
Feria Artesanal de
la Recoleta, 92

Feria Central de Artesanos (Mar de Plata), 121
Feria de Artisanias (Tilcara), 164
Feria de Neuquén, 184
Feria del Productor al Consumidor (La Rioja), 221
Feria del Pulgadas Peru 38 (Paraná), 114
Ferias, 231
Fernández de Kirchner, Cristina, 59, 61–62
Festival Ciudad Emergente (Buenos Aires), 50
Festivals, 50–51, 98, 100, 129, 150, 159, 161, 165, 219
Fiesta de la Chaya (La Rioja), 219
Fiesta de la Quebrada (Humahuaca), 165
Films, Argentina in, 52
Fishing, 182, 200
Flea markets, 38, 82, 114, 121
Florida Street (El Centro), 95
Fly fishing, 182
Food, 138–139, 142, 231–244
carne, 236
mate, 65–67
mediacena, 215
menu items, 234–236
recipes, 238–244
street, 37, 209
vegetarian, 160, 231–232
Food Bank Foundation (Buenos Aires), 226
Formosa, 132–133
Fossils, 162
Futbol (soccer), 63, 213

G
Gaiman, 206
Garganta de Diablo (Tilcara), 162
Gauchos, 64
Gay and lesbian travelers, 51, 68, 252
General Belgrano bridge (Corrientes), 130
General Paz (Córdoba), 98
Geothermal spas (Cólon), 116
Glaciarium (El Calafate), 196, 197
Glaciers, walking on, 174, 179
Gondola, 139–140
Gonzalez Caro, Luchi, 247–249
Graffiti Tours (Buenos Aires), 80
Greetings, 57–58, 63
Gualeguaychu

Carnival de Pais, 50
Güemes (Córdoba), 98
Guerrero Chocolates (El Calafate), 199
Guevara, Ernesto "Che," 99, 105
Gutekunst, Kristin, 250–252

H
Handcraft markets, 97, 103. See also Craft fairs
Health, 23–35, 248–249
Argentine pharmacies, 27–28
bed bugs, 28–29
birth control, 26
malaria and dengue fever, 24–25
pregnancy termination, 25–26
Q&As, 30–35
sexually transmitted diseases, 26
tampons, 27
toilet paper, 27
vaccinations and medications, 24
women's clinics, 23
Helideria Miranda (Cafayate), 143
Hiking
Jujuy province, 159, 165–166
La Cumbrecita, 100

Patagonia, 178, 179, 186–187
Hill of Seven Colors, 153, 159
Historic homes, 119
History museums, 87, 99, 131
Hitchhiking, 186
Holidays, 43
Horse riding, 197
Humahuaca, 162, 165–167

I

Ice-climbing, 197
Ice cream, shopping for, 181
Iglesia de San Jose (Cachi), 146
Iguazu Falls, 123, 125–126
In Patagonia (Bruce Chatwin), 52
Inca ruins, 162, 166
Inmaculanda Concepcion del Belgrano, 86
International Travelers Information (CDC), 10
Internet access, 45
Irish pub (Mendoza), 218
Iruya, 147–149
Isla Bridges (Ushuaia), 203
Isla de Hornos, 116

J

Jeep tours, 197
Jewelry, 13

Jujuy province, 153–169
accommodations, 157–160, 163, 167, 169
activities, 157, 159, 162, 165–166, 169
Humahuaca, 165–167
Purmamarca, 159–160
San Salvador de Jujuy, 156–158
shopping, 158, 160, 164, 167, 169
Tilcara, 160–164
top picks, 153
travel tips, 156, 159–161, 165, 168
Tucuman, 168–169

K

Kayaking, 107–108, 179
Kirchner, Néstor, 59

L

La Boca (Buenos Aires), 80
La Boutique de las Artesanias (Cólon), 118
La Casa Rosada (El Centro), 93
La Cumbrecita, 97, 99–100, 102
La Fiesta Nacional del Pancho (Catamarca), 150
La Florida (Rosario), 107

La Garganta del Diablo (Cafayate), 143
La Iglesia de Santa Rosa (Purmamarca), 159
La Recoleta Cemetery, 90
La Redonda (Belgrano), 86
La Ribera (Santa Fe), 112
La Rioja, 219–221
La Trochita train ride (Esquel), 192
La Virgen del Valle Cathedral (Catamarca), 151
Lago Epuyen, 189–191
Lago Puelo, 186
Laguna Tortora (San Cosme), 130
Las Malvinas, 62, 63
Lentil Stew (recipe), 240
A Lexicon of Terror (Marguerite Feitlowit), 52
L.I.F.E. Argentina (Buenos Aires), 225–226
Litoral, 123–133
accommodations, 126–128, 131, 133
activities, 125–126, 130–131
Corrientes, 129–131
Formosa, 132–133
Puerto Iguazú, 123–128

shopping, 128, 131, 133
top picks, 123
transportation, 125
travel tips, 125, 129–130, 132
Local, Q&A with, 247–249
Los Glaciares National Park, 196, 197

M

Machismo culture, 14, 17–18
Magellan penguins, 206
Maipu, 213, 215
Malaria, 24–25
MALBA (Buenos Aires), 81
Malls, 102, 109, 112
Mama Goye (San Carlos de Bariloche), 181
Mamuska (San Carlos de Bariloche), 181
Manzana Jesuitica (Córdoba), 99
Mar de Plata, 106, 118–121
Markets. See also Craft fairs
antique, 89
Buenos Aires, 38, 82, 87, 89, 92
Córdoba, 103
Cuyo, 217, 221
Entre Rios, 114,

121
flea, 38, 82, 114, 121
handcraft, 97, 103
Jujuy province, 158, 164
Patagonia, 177–178, 181
Salta province, 141, 151
Mate, 65–67, 106, 114, 188, 248
Mediacena, 215
Medications, 24, 28
Mendoza, 11, 37, 209, 212–218
Mendoza Wine Connection, 215
Menu items, 234–236
Mercado de Pulgas
Mar de Plata, 121
Palermo, 38, 82
Mercado San Miguel (Salta), 141
Metro, 78, 79
Metropolitan Cathedral (El Centro), 93
Money, protecting your, 39
Monpelat, Silvina, 32–35
Monumento a los Héroes de la Independencia (Humahuaca), 166
Monumento His-

torico Nacional a la Bandera (Rosario), 107
Morning-after pill, 26
The Motorcycle Diaries (film), 52
Mount Fitz Roy, 193, 194
Mr. Hugo's Wineries and Bikes (Mendoza), 209, 213
Museo Arqueologico Adan Quiroga (Catamarca), 151
Museo Arqueológico Municipal (Humahuaca), 166
Museo de Arte Contemporáneo (Santa Fe), 111
Museo de Arte Latinoamericano de Buenos Aires, 81
Museo de Arte Sacro (La Rioja), 220
Museo de la Vid y el Vino (Cafayate), 143
Museo del Hielo Patagonia (El Calafate), 197
Museo del Mar (Mar de Plata), 119
Museo del Presidio (Ushuaia), 202

Museo Ernesto
Che Guevara
(Córdoba), 99
Museo Historico
de Corrientes,
131
Museo Historico
Nacional (San
Telmo), 87
Museo Maritimi
(Ushuaia), 202
Museo Único del
Mate (Paraná),
114
Music, 51, 160
Mustard trick
(scam), 19

N
National Beer Fes-
tival (Córdoba),
51
National Flag Me-
morial (Rosario),
107
National parks
El Parque Nacio-
nal del Tierra del
Fuego (Ushuaia),
203
El Parque Nacio-
nal Los Alceres,
189, 192
Los Glaciares
National Park,
196, 197
Parque Nacional
Los Cardones
(Cachi), 146
Parque Nacional
Palmar (Cólon),
116
National Reorga-
nization Process,

60
Navegando el Fin
del Mundo, 203
Neuquén, 182–184
Night, traveling at,
75
Northeastern
Argentina. see
Litoral
Northern Argentin-
ean Army, 166
Nueva Córdoba,
98, 102
Nueve Reinas
(film), 52

O
Obelisk (El
Centro), 93
Office of Overseas
Citizens Services,
10
Oktoberfest (Villa
General Bel-
grano), 100
Old Patagonian
Express, 192

P
Packing list, 46–47
Paleontology
museums, 182–
183, 206–207
Palermo (Buenos
Aires), 23, 74,
82–84
Panaderia Juan
Julio (El Cala-
fate), 199
Panchos, 150
Paraguay, 132,
133
Paraná, 106,
113–115

Parque General
San Martin
(Mendoza), 213
Parque Indepen-
dencia (Rosario),
107
Parque Nacional
Los Cardones
(Cachi), 146
Parque Nacional
Palmar (Cólon),
116
Parque San Martin
(Salta), 141
Parque Sarmiento
(Córdoba), 99
Paseo de Artesa-
nias (San Salva-
dor de Jujuy),
158
Paseo Garganta
de Diablo
(Iguazu Falls),
126
Paseo Inferior
(Iguazu Falls),
126
Paso de la Patria
(Corrientes), 131
Patagonia, 45,
171–207
accommodations,
179–181, 183–
184, 187–188,
190, 192–193,
195, 198–200,
203–204, 207
activities, 178–179,
182–183, 186–
187, 189–190,
192, 194, 197,
200–203, 206–207
El Bolson, 185–188
El Calafate,

196–199
El Chalten, 193–195
Esquel, 191–193
Lago Epuyen and Trevelin, 189–191
Neuquén, 182–184
Rio Gallegos, 200–201
San Carlos de Bariloche, 176–181
shopping, 181, 184, 188, 191, 195, 199, 205
top picks, 174
transportation, 176–177, 182, 185, 189, 191, 194, 196, 202, 205
travel tips, 177–178, 182, 185–186, 189, 191, 197, 202, 206
Trelew, 205–207
Ushuaia, 201–205
Patio Olmos (Córdoba), 102
Patricio Peralta Ramos Boulevard (Mar de Plata), 119
Peatonal Junin (Corrientes), 129, 131
Peñas Blancas (Humahuaca), 165–166
Penguins, 200–201, 206

People watching, 111
Perito Moreno, 174, 197
Permaculture volunteer programs, 228
Perón, Eva "Evita," 51, 58, 90
Perón, Isabel Martinez de, 58
Perón, Juan Domingo, 58–59
Peso, 38
Pharmacies, Argentine, 27–28
Pickpockets, 19
Planning your travel, 12
Plas y Coed (Gaiman), 206
Playa Grande (Mar de Plata), 119
Plaza de Belgrano (San Salvador de Jujuy), 157
Plaza de la República (El Centro), 93
Plaza de Mayo (El Centro), 93
Plaza Dorrego (San Telmo), 87
Plaza Espana (Mendoza), 213
Plaza Independencia (Mendoza), 217
Plaza 9 de Julio (Salta), 141
Plaza Serrano

(Palermo), 84
Police, 68–69
Politics, 61–63, 153, 156
Por una cabeza (song), 44
Pregnancy termination, 25–26, 34–35, 249
Public holidays, 43
Pucará de Tilcara, 162
Pueblos, 138
Puerto Iguazú, 123–128
Puerto Madero (Buenos Aires), 81
Puerto Madryn, 45, 174
Punta Iglesia (Mar de Plata), 119
Punta Tombo (Trelew), 206
Purmamarca, 153, 159–160
Purses, 47

Q
Quebrada de Humahuaca, 165
Quinquela Martin, Benito, 80

R
Radio Taxis, 12, 48
Recoleta (Buenos Aires), 23, 90–92
Red Solidaria

(Buenos Aires),
226–227
Religion, 57
Restaurants, 218.
See also Food
Retiro (Buenos
Aires), 92–95
Rio Gallegos,
200–201
Río Uruguay, 116
River Paraná,
107–108, 111
River Plate, 63
Rosario, 105–109
Ruins, Inca, 162,
166
Ruta 40, driving,
175

S
Safe Abortion
Hotline, 35
Safety, 9–20, 39
appropriate dress,
20
in Buenos Aires,
74–75
on buses, 15–17
catcalls, 14–15
Córdoba, 98
emergency ser-
vices, 11
machismo culture,
17–18
protecting be-
longings, 18–19
protecting money,
39
resources, 10
safety tips, 12–14
scams, 19–20
solo travel, 9–10
Tourist Police Unit,
11

U.S. embassies
and consulates,
20
Salinas Grandes
(Salta), 138, 139
Salta (city), 37,
135–141
Salta province, 24,
135–151
accommodations,
140, 143–144,
146, 148–149, 151
activities, 139–140,
143, 146, 148,
151
Cachi, 145–146
Cafayate, 142–144
Catamarca,
149–151
Iruya, 147–149
Salta, 135–141
shopping, 141,
144, 149, 151
top picks, 138
transportation,
138, 145, 147
travel tips, 138–
139, 142–143,
145, 148, 150
San Carlos de Bari-
loche, 176–181
San Cosme, 123,
130–131
San Isidro, 148, 149
San Miguel de
Tucuman,
168–169
San Salvador
de Jujuy, 153,
156–158
San Telmo (Buenos
Aires), 74, 87–89
Santa Fe, 110–112
Sarmiento Street

(Mendoza), 217
Scams, 19–20, 75
Scooters, 129
Sculpture park,
186–187
Secure taxis, 20
Security, in Buenos
Aires, 74–75
Semana Musical
Llao Llao (San
Carlos de Bari-
loche), 51
SET Idiomas
(Córdoba),
227–228
Sex and sexuality,
in culture, 68
Sexually transmit-
ted diseases
(STDs), 26
Shopping
Buenos Aires, 38,
74, 82, 84, 86, 89,
92, 95
Córdoba, 97,
102–103
Cuyo, 217, 221
Entre Rios, 109,
112, 115, 118,
121
Jujuy, 158, 160,
164, 167, 169
Litoral, 128, 131,
133
Patagonia, 181,
184, 188, 191,
195, 199, 205
Salta province,
141, 144, 149,
151
Skiing, 190
Skydiving, 98
Slashed bag
scam, 19–20

Smart Traveler Enrollment Program, 10
Smoking, 47
Soccer, 63, 213
Solidarity Network (Buenos Aires), 226–227
Solo travel, 9–10
Spanish language, 12, 40, 255–261
classes, 227–228
greetings, 58
medications, 28
slang, 15, 260–261
Spinach and Ricotta Tart (recipe), 244
STDs (sexually transmitted diseases), 26
Street food, 37, 209
Subte, 78, 79
Super Pancho, 209, 214–215
Supermarkets, 188
Surfing, 106, 119

T

Talleres de Cerámica (Humahuaca), 167
Tampons, 27, 178
Tango, 44, 50, 138
Tango Piola, 44
Taxis, 47–48, 75
in Buenos Aires, 78

Radio, 12, 48
secure, 20
Tea houses, 206
Teatro Colón (El Centro), 93
Teatro 3 de Febrero (Paraná), 113–114
Teleferico (Salta), 139–140
Temperatures
daytime, 106, 125
nighttime, 145, 168
Termas Cachueta (Mendoza), 209, 215
Termas de Cólon, 116
Theaters, 93, 113–114
Tickets, bus, 15
Tigre, 228
Tilcara, 37, 153, 160–164
Tilcara Carnival Festival, 50
Toilet paper, 27
Toiletries, 178
Tourist cards, 49
Tourist Police Unit, 11
Tours
bicycle, 80, 143, 209, 213–214
boat, 107–108, 111, 113, 126, 203
Buenos Aires, 80
Cabo Vírgenes, 200–201
Cachi, 145
eco-, 115

El Calafate, 197
islands near Cólon, 116
jeep, 197
Salinas Grandes (Salta), 139
Ventisquero Negro (San Carlos de Bariloche), 179
wineries and vineyards, 213–216
Trains, 48, 78, 192
Transportation, 47–48
Buenos Aires, 78–79
Cuyo, 212
Entre Rios, 106, 110, 113, 115, 119
Litoral, 125
Patagonia, 176–177, 182, 185, 189, 191, 194, 196, 202, 205
Salta province, 138, 145, 147
Travel Blogs, Argentina-inspired, 53
Travel season, 45, 176, 178, 206
Trekking, 38, 187, 194, 197
Trelew, 205–207
Trevelin, 189–191
Tucuman, 168–169
Ty Cymraeg (Gaiman), 206

U

Uco Valley, 213–215
Union de los Pibes (Buenos Aires), 225
Uruguay, 115
U.S. consulates, 10, 20
U.S. Department of State, 10
U.S. embassies, 10, 20, 82
Ushuaia, 201–205

V

Vaccinations, 24
Vegetarian food, 160, 231–232
Ventisquero Negro (San Carlos de Bariloche), 179
Video format, 45
Views
Andes Mountains, 148
Cascada de los Duendes (San Carlos de Bariloche), 179
Cerrado Campanario, 178
Cerro de Los Siete Colores, 153
El Chalten, 193
Garganta de Diablo (Tilcara), 162
General Belgrano bridge (Corrientes), 130
Iguazu Falls, 123, 125–126
Lago Puelo, 186

Mendoza, 213
Peñas Blancas (Humahuaca), 165–166
Salinas Grandes (Salta), 138, 139
Villa Fatalaufquen (Lago Epuyen), 189
Villa General Belgrano, 100
Visas, 49
Voluntario Global (Buenos Aires), 227
Volunteer programs, 223–228
agriculture and permaculture, 228
animal welfare, 228
in Buenos Aires, 95
community outreach, 226–228
teaching English, 223
working with children, 225–226

W

Waikiki beach (Mar de Plata), 119
Walking
Buenos Aires, 78
Cachi, 146
on glaciers, 174, 179
safety tips, 13
San Isidro, 148
Tucuman, 148
Waterfalls, 100, 179

Weather, 45, 202, 212
Welsh settlements, 190
Whale watching, 45, 174
Wine, 37, 142, 183, 209, 213–215
Women's clinics, 23, 35
WOOFing, 186

Y

Yok Wahi Bar (San Salvador de Jujuy), 157